THE ORIENT EXPRESS

0 50 100 150 300 400
MILES

BERLIN
N Y
WARS
POLAND
PRAGUE
CZECHOSLOVAKIA
inz
DANUBE
Vienna
Bratislava
USSR
I A
Nove Zamky
Budapest
HUNGARY
AGREB
Subotica
Szeged
RUMANIA
Timisoara (Temesvar)
SAVA
Novi Sad
YUGOSLAVIA
Belgrade
Sinaia
Ploesti
Craiova
Bucharest
DANUBE
Giurgevo
Roustchouk
Nisch
Pirot
BULGARIA
Sofia
VARNA
Ikhtiman
BLACK SEA
Tatar-Bazardjik
MARITZA
ALBANIA
GREECE
Tscherkesskuy (Tcherkuy)
S E A
ISTANBUL
TURKEY

Orient Express

Garry Hogg

ORIENT EXPRESS

The Birth, Life and Death of a Great Train

Walker and Company • New York

First published in the United States of America in 1969 by Walker and Company, a division of the Walker Publishing Company, Inc.

Library of Congress Catalog
Card Number: 77-79384

Printed in the United States of America from type set in Great Britain.

Contents

Illustrations

[Numbers 11, 14, 16 and 17 by courtesy of *La Vie du Rail Photograph*]

Author's Note

I should like to thank two people in particular for the great help they were to me during the month of May, 1964, when I was preparing to write this book. They are M. Roger Commault, a retired servant of La Compagnie Internationale des Wagons-Lits et des Grands Express Européens, and Madame C. Lurie, still a valued servant of the Company.

M. Roger Commault generously gave me permission to look through his unique collection of engravings and photographs relating to the Orient Express, and to use as many of them as I liked. He also answered innumerable questions about 'the old days' when he served aboard the train, and produced a wealth of rare material of which he had photostat copies made for me.

Madame Lurie generously let me occupy a corner of her Paris office for days on end while I was researching through the Company's archives, and answered all the countless questions I put to her without ever suggesting for one moment that I might be a nuisance.

Without their willing, intelligent and imaginative co-operation I should never have been able to write the sort of book I feel so remarkable a train as the Orient Express deserves by way of commemorative tribute.

* * *

Merci, Monsieur et Madame, mille fois!

G.H.

I

Brain-child

On a certain Wednesday morning in the year 1883 careful readers of *The Times* may have spotted a small paragraph on page ten, column two. It ran as follows:

> On last Friday evening at 7.30 the new quick railway service between Paris and Constantinople, via Vienna and Giurgevo, came into operation. For the present it will be a bi-weekly service both ways, leaving Paris at half-past 7 p.m. on Tuesdays and Fridays; and the train will consist of three saloon carriages, fitted with 42 beds, a refreshment saloon, and a sufficient number of luggage vans, in which the luggage will be so arranged that it can be examined in the vans by the Customs officers at the frontier stations, thus avoiding the delay and annoyance unavoidable when the luggage has to be removed from the train. There will be no change of carriages between Paris and Giurgevo, and it is expected that the entire journey between Paris and Constantinople will be completed in about 75 hours.

Very few readers will have done more than skim casually through the paragraph about the new train service. Railways were no longer a novelty; thousands of miles of track criss-crossed Europe; what was one new train, anyway, even if it did seem to be going to travel over a longer rail route than any already in existence?

In fact, that is just what was remarkable about the train referred to in that brief paragraph: it was to be the very first European transcontinental express. Though, thanks to men like the great George Stephenson, railways had their origin in Europe, it was the Americans who had built the world's first transcontinental railroad—the famous 'Union Pacific'. That had been fifteen years before. As so often, Europe gave the lead, and then lagged behind.

For all that, the new transcontinental express so briefly referred to in that tiny paragraph was before very long to become one of the most famous trains in the world, and to remain so for eighty-odd years. An enthusiastic Frenchman, when he first made its acquaintance, dubbed it 'The Magic Carpet to the East'; the owners gave it a title which still, after all these years and all the new developments in long-distance travel, has the power to fire the imagination: 'The Orient Express'.

This is the train that was the setting for Alfred Hitchcock's thriller film, *The Lady Vanishes*; it was the 'hero', so to speak, of Carol Reed's great film, *The Night Train*; it appeared again in Graham Greene's breathless novel, *Stamboul Train*. Writers of crime and detective fiction, like Agatha Christie, Simenon, Eric Ambler and Leslie Charteris, have used it in their trans-European spy chases. In real life it has been used by emperors and crooks, by diplomats and maharajahs, by millionaires and dubious financiers, by adventurers and adventuresses, by abdicating monarchs and by famous men and women attempting for reasons of their own to travel *incognito*. Over the years the Orient Express has surrounded itself with an aura of drama and intrigue and mystery and the very smell of the East. The newspaper reporter who sent in that small paragraph about the new train little knew how famous it was to become!

The Orient Express—or *Express d'Orient*, as it was first called—was the brain-child of a Belgian engineer named Georges Nagelmackers, a man of vision and a dynamic personality. Portraits of him in his heyday show him as a splendid figure standing close to six feet tall—a good height for a Belgian—and broad in proportion. Beneath his noble brow is a pair of piercing eyes. He sports the flowing moustache, side-whiskers and massive beard of his era, and the frock-coat, double-breasted white waistcoat and beautifully brushed silver-grey top hat and cane which he always carried mark him out as a man of distinction who could hold his own in any company, however important.

His profession of engineer had led him, while still in his early twenties, to America. There he had been immensely impressed by the high standards of comfort, as well as efficiency in running, to be found on the rapidly expanding American railroad system. He was there at the very time when the great Union Pacific Railroad between Omaha and Sacramento, linking the Pacific with the Atlantic, was nearing completion. It may well have been this great enterprise that fired his determination to organise in Europe a project that would be comparable with the American one.

He did not plan to build a railway: there were already plenty of these in Europe, criss-crossing the continent from west to east and north to south, owned by a number of independent national authorities, from France in the west by way of Germany and Austria to Rumania in the east. What Nagelmackers determined to do was to revolutionise the conditions of travel over this network by reproducing, and, if possible, improving upon, the standards he had found in the United States. Above all he was going to concern himself with long-distance travel, for the benefit of diplomats and businessmen whose occupations involved them in crossing frontiers and so spending several successive nights cooped up in uncomfortable railway-trains.

True, the European trains of the 1870s were a great improvement on the 'cattle-trucks' of a few decades before, in the early days of rail travel; but they were still often grimly uncomfortable. One regular long-distance traveller of those days was pretty outspoken on the subject:

> The wagons [he wrote] are lit by a small window or two, which are virtually impossible to open, and are always thick with dust. They are hardly better than a poor type of ship's cabin on wheels, a mobile prison-cell. . . . A man needs to be able to stretch his legs, expand his chest, flex his elbows. I have looked out through the window of my compartment and seen, drawn up beneath some hedgerow, a circus caravan in which a whole family, father, mother and countless children lived, ate their meals, drank their wine, and slept serenely. I envied them the comparative spaciousness of their mobile home!

This was the sort of complaint Nagelmackers had heard many times. Listening to such complaints, his thoughts turned to the American sleeping-cars, the invention of a man named George Pullman, who was to give his name to the most popular type of railway coach on our own railway system today. Pullman had designed an ingenious arrangement by which the daytime coaches could be converted to night-time use. The tables between the seats were removed, the seats lowered and the space between them filled in; so, a sort of bed resulted. Curtains were drawn along rods that ran the full length of the coach on each side of the central aisle. This turned the whole coach into a sort of long, narrow dormitory made up of two rows of makeshift beds placed end to end and hidden behind them.

Georges Nagelmackers, however, resolved to produce something better than this. Not for him the American-style 'dormitory': passengers using his coach should have the sort of privacy they were accustomed to in their homes and the better-class hotels. He would design a type of sleeping-car that would be welcomed by the affluent passenger for whom only the best was good enough. Being an engineer by profession, he was a thoroughly practical man; he was also, as it happened, a man of imagination.

By our standards the coaches he designed were hardly more than toys. They were just over twenty-nine feet long and had only four wheels, whereas many of our coaches today are fitted with two six-wheel bogies: twelve wheels in all, on six axles. Each coach consisted of three compartments and a corridor. Each compartment contained four well-upholstered easy-chairs which could be drawn together, their backs let down, and so form a comfortable bed. Halfway up the walls were two bunks. These were hinged and could be lowered by pulleys until they hung level from ropes attached to the ceiling, to accommodate the passengers who were not using the chair-beds. The American-style 'dormitory' coach was thus replaced by three bedrooms-for-four, private and intimate. In the corridor there were two wash-basins and two enclosed W.C.s, one reserved for Ladies, the other for Gentlemen. In addition there was a stove with a boiler to provide heating for the coach generally and hot water for the passengers to use in the basins.

Nagelmackers had not a great deal of money available for his project, and was obliged at first to throw in his lot with an American named William Mann who had come over to Europe with a design of his own. He called it 'The Mann Boudoir Sleeping Car', and he was proud to have his photograph taken sitting on the running-board of one of his cars, with the impressive Georges Nagelmackers standing beside him. Both are wearing the conventional top hats and frock-coats of the day. For some reason, the Belgian for once is supporting himself not by his customary silver-knobbed cane but by an umbrella. So proud was William Mann of his creation that he had the initial 'M' engraved on the window section of each compartment door. He had reason for pride: his Boudoir Sleeping Car had three axles, six wheels, to Nagelmacker's two axles and four wheels.

Mann sensed after a short while that he was unlikely to get very far alongside so dominant a personality as the Belgian engineer, so he astutely sold him the rolling-stock he had already built, and returned to America. From that moment onwards Georges Nagelmackers, engineer of vision, had the field wide open, without a single competitor in sight.

His aim now was to put as many of his sleeping-cum-dining-cars (for this was the project nearest to his heart) on to the network of European railways as he could persuade the various railway companies to accept. He had no intention of running railways of his own, but simply to supply existing companies with the sort of rolling-stock that would provide luxury for the ever-mounting numbers of long-distance passengers now buying tickets for places all over the Continent. They must sleep in comfort, eat in comfort, travel in comfort; and he alone could bring this about.

He formed a company to build this new-style railway coach and to organise and promote distribution. He gave it the resounding title: '*Compagnie Internationale des Wagons-Lits*'. That title is used to this day, almost a century after its inauguration; but now it has been lengthened by five more words. Running the full length of every coach making up these giant trans-European express trains, wherever they may be bound, are the words: *Compagnie Internationale des Wagons-Lits et des Grands Express Européens.*

It was from the Gare de l'Est, Paris, that the majority of the newly planned long-distance European expresses would be starting their journeys. They would be operated by the *Compagnie de l'Est.* Fortunately for Georges Nagelmackers this railway company was forward-looking and enterprising as well as firmly established. It was aware that the longest-distance train of all those projected, bound for the East—with all that that implied!—would leave from its Paris terminus, on the eastern outskirts of the city. From the Gare de l'Est would leave a new train, bound for Constantinople (as today's Istanbul was then called). It would pass over no fewer than seven independent rail networks beyond France; it would cross no fewer than seven frontiers; its terminus would be almost two thousand miles east of Paris, and some eighty hours' travelling-time distant. Its name, fittingly, would be *Express d'Orient.*

Maps of Europe drawn eighty-odd years ago show not only a very different and more complex set of frontiers but an extraordinary pattern of railways, each under a different authority. Some of these were already complete; others had been broken off short where, for instance, a mountain range or wide river or area of marsh had presented an obstacle too great to tackle with equipment then at the engineers' disposal. There were mountains and hills and rugged valleys and high plateaux and swamps and thick forest belts: every railway company had its own problems. It was not only Nagelmackers' newly formed Company that had difficulties to face and conquer. But the problem of persuading individual companies to see things Nagelmackers' way was one that took a lot of solving.

The track operated by the Compagnie de l'Est joined that operated by The Imperial Management of the Alsace-Lorraine Railways. Beyond this came the State Railways of the Grand Duchy of Baden, The State Railways of the Kingdom of Württemberg, The Lines of Communication of the Kingdom of Bavaria (all these being independent authorities within the vast country of Germany). Then came Austria, with two rival railway companies: The State Railways of Vienna, and The Imperial and Royal Austrian State Railways Company. Hungary was included among them, for in those days it was part of the Austro-Hungarian Empire. Finally there was The Royal General Management of the Rumanian Railways, almost at the end of the newly projected long-distance route. And there were still Bulgaria, and Turkey, further east again.

It was one thing to design and construct these sleeper- and dining-cars, and to persuade a number of independent railway authorities to allow them to be run over their tracks; it was another to popularise them, to let the prospective passenger know what was being offered to him when he embarked henceforward on long-distance travel. But without publicity this new venture might die almost before it was brought to life. Nagelmackers decided to concentrate on the child of his dreams, the first trans-European express, the train that was to link France with Turkey. He would publicise it in every way he knew.

He had numbers of large posters displayed in Paris, in London, in Brussels, in Vienna, in Constantinople itself. These clearly and emphatically announced the inception of this new service between West and East. Every poster was boldly emblazoned with the letters 'O-E' in the colours of the Ottoman Empire (as Turkey was then known). These were just the preliminary announcements.

But something more than posters and newspaper advertisements was necessary if the new project was to catch the imagination (and the purses) of the travelling public, the diplomats and business executives, the moneyed men (and women too) who had the means and leisure to travel widely without any purpose other than to amuse themselves. There was no cinema, no television advertising in those far-off days. Yet something spectacular was called for if the project of trans-European travel was to become a talking-point over a whole continent. Nagelmackers was something more than a distinguished engineer; he was a man of imagination and vision. It was he who thought up the notion of the great Inaugural Run of the Orient Express.

2

'En Voiture!'

Dusk had already fallen over Paris in the late afternoon of 4th October, 1883. It was thickening into darkness among the narrow streets and unlit alleys of the *dixième arrondissement* in which was to be found the Gare de l'Est.

It was not a salubrious neighbourhood. The inhabitants lived within earshot of shrill whistling, the strident blowing-off of steam from impatient locomotives, the endless clanking of shunting wagons being coupled and uncoupled and marshalled in the sidings that ran parallel with the granite-cobbled streets. They breathed air made foul by the reek of fumes from the gas-works and the clouds of acrid, greasy smoke belching from the chimneys of locomotives burning the dirty coal *briquettes* of the day. The Gare de l'Est was the focal point of their district. Many of the men who lived there worked in the engine sheds and on the sidings, as cleaners, shunters, porters, coal-heavers, permanent-way men. Their wives fought an unceasing battle to keep their small homes clean against the invasion of coal-dust and smoke, their permanent enemy.

There were no 'train-spotters' in those days. But idlers who had nothing better to do that late afternoon than stand about gossiping and watch the coming and going of passengers became vaguely conscious of an atmosphere of subdued excitement building up beneath the station roof, as of some impending event of note. Behind the hiss of escaping steam and the rattle of porters' trolleys their ears caught the clip-clop of horses' hooves as a succession of Paris *fiacres*, and a private carriage or two, trundled briskly into the station forecourt, following one another at unusually short intervals.

Passengers buying their tickets and carefully counting their change beneath the uncertain light penetrating the smoky air from the scattered lamps overhead became aware that there were other passengers, passengers obviously more privileged than themselves, who were passing the ticket-office without so much as turning their heads, and making straight for the barrier of the main departure platform used by the longer-distance trains rather than by the suburban ones. Why, they probably asked themselves a little resentfully, should other intending passengers be so much more privileged than they were? Did they not have to buy tickets for their journey?

A possible answer to the question that nagged at them lay in the appearance of these privileged passengers. They swept in a lordly fashion through the booking-hall with the greatest assurance. They wore long, fashionably tailored, velvet or astrakhan-collared greatcoats and tall, immaculately brushed silk hats. Several of them were followed by manservants who walked with one hand on the trolleys pushed by the station porters, loaded high with baggage: a round-topped trunk, a bulky hold-all in which thick travelling-rugs were strapped into a massive roll, a shaped leather hat-box, and miscellaneous hand-luggage. Here and there a gilded monogram glinted on the dark leather. It was evident at a glance that these were men of importance.

Those who took the trouble to follow these distinguished-looking passengers noticed that as each stepped on to the departure platform he was greeted individually by a succession of equally distinguished-looking gentlemen also wearing greatcoats and tall silk hats. Something out of the ordinary was obviously afoot; this was something of an occasion.

An occasion it most certainly was. This was the beginning of the official inaugural run of the new luxury train, the Orient Express, designed to link Paris, capital of France, with Constantinople, the capital of the remote Ottoman Empire. To mark the occasion, four important personages, members of the newly formed Compagnie Internationale des Wagons-Lits and its backers, were acting as joint hosts to a mixed party of some forty diplomats, publicists and pressmen whom they had invited to be their guests on this, the new luxury train's official inaugural run. (The train had already been run, some months before, unofficially and without any advertising, as much as anything to check the rail system and work out the timing between point and point: this had been pure routine.)

The four representatives of the Company stood there, waiting to greet each of their guests in turn. First and foremost, M. Georges Nagelmackers, founder of the Company and promoter of the whole enterprise. Beside him stood his deputy, M. Napoleon Schroeder. Flanking them stood two influential Belgian bankers whose money had been put into the Company: Messieurs Delloye-Matthieu and Lechat.

And now for their guests. One by one they passed the barrier, their gilt-edged invitation-cards in their hands, and made themselves known to their hosts. From the Embassy in Paris of the Ottoman Empire came its First Secretary, Missak-Effendi. He was a widely travelled man who spoke a number of languages, including, of course, French. He had been appointed to the Embassy because he was the sort of man who could be relied upon to forge sound links between the diplomats and merchants of West and East. Nagelmackers had invited him to ensure that his new project, this brain-child of his, would have the full backing of someone influential in both countries.

Next to arrive was Belgium's Minister of Public Works, M. Olin, a younger man of great ability and promise. Close behind him came M. Dubois, General Manager of the Belgian State Railways. France, too, was naturally well represented. The French Minister of Finance deputed his Chief Controller, M. Grimpel, to represent him. And each of the independent French railway companies had been invited to send representatives.

Possibly more important in Nagelmackers' eyes were the carefully selected publicity men, well-known journalists of several nationalities. The French national press was represented by three young and alert men: M. Tréfeu, of *Le Gaulois*, M. Boyer, and M. Daudet. There were one or two German newspapermen. And though the route was to run far to the south of the Netherlands, there was a Dutch journalist named Janszen who, in spite of his country's reputation for stolidity and lack of humour, proved to be the life and soul of the party. Even more than the diplomats and the railway representatives, it was men such as these on whom Nagelmackers was astutely relying for publicity.

Better known, however, than any of these newspapermen were two Special Correspondents, incidentally authors, veterans in their chosen sphere of activity. One of these was M. Oppen de Blowitz, European Correspondent of *The Times*; the other was M. Edmond About, author and controversialist, a native of Alsace who had been an exile in France for the past twelve years, ever since the Germans had occupied his native land. Both men wrote books about this famous journey from Paris to Constantinople. Because they were very different types of men their books were written from rather different standpoints. M. About was a man of wit and discernment. He filled his book with vivid descriptions of places passed through, people he met, things that happened to this intrepid party of long-distance travellers; and incidentally with needle-sharp character-sketches of his fellow-passengers—including Oppen de Blowitz, whom he appears not much to have liked.

At length the party was complete. Or at any rate practically so, for as yet there were no representatives of Austro-Hungary, through so much of whose territory the route lay. This deficiency was to be made good when the train pulled in, first at Strasbourg and later at Vienna, and again at Budapest, in Hungary. M. About was pleased to learn that the all-male party which composed the passenger-list in the Gare de l'Est was going to be able to welcome aboard at these stations not only the Austro-Hungarian officials but also some of their wives.

Now the whole assembled party was standing about on the low platform alongside the track. As yet there was no sign of the train which they had been invited to board by those gilt-edged cards sent to them all individually by the

President of the Company. The only specimen of rolling-stock in evidence was one of the ancient and dilapidated sleeping-cars which for some years past had been attached to one of the few long-distance trains already running. It was the type of coach that had been referred to by that jaundiced traveller as a 'ship's cabin on wheels, a mobile prison-cell'.

M. About, for one, stared somewhat grimly at it. He was among the most experienced rail travellers in the party and had suffered long and often aboard these primitive 'sleepers'. Not only were they cramped, but they were mounted on harshly sprung axles, and only two of these, so that the coach was jolted badly at every rail joint and the unhappy passengers were tossed about like the proverbial peas in a pan. The dim and flickering oil lamps made reading almost impossible. The heating was almost non-existent, for the man responsible for stoking the boiler was often surly and had to be continually 'sweetened' by frequent tips. M. About fingered his invitation-card and told himself that if something very much more attractive than that ancient sleeper was not to be his lot, then he would stay behind and leave the others to suffer as he himself had so often suffered in the past!

Just as he was thinking this, a sound was heard which made him and everyone else on the platform turn his head in one direction. Backing into the Gare de l'Est from the darkness of the tunnel beyond came the rearward coach of the new train. Against the dark background from which it was emerging, and even beneath the lighting of the station itself, it shone and sparkled like a Christmas tree lit by fairy lights. A ripple of excitement ran through the party standing waiting for it: the moment had at last come when they were to see for the first time the fabulous train on which they had been invited to be the first privileged guests.

Coach after coach backed slowly in towards them from the darkness, throwing vivid shafts of light across the platform. Sightseers crowding by the barrier let out gasps of astonishment. Even the hard-bitten railwaymen, and the dignified bankers and diplomats, found it difficult to restrain themselves from expressions of enthusiasm. M. About wrote of the coaches, and certainly not in bitterness this time, as 'mobile homes, constructed of teak and glass, brilliantly lit by gas lamps, splendidly windowed, as well appointed and comfortable, on immediate view, as any luxury flat in Paris'. He was so interested in the brilliant lighting of the coaches as, one after another, they were backed into the station that he failed to notice that they were mounted not on two axles, or even three, but—for the first time—on bogies. His colleague, Oppen de Blowitz, placed it on record that on this inaugural run of the Orient Express he found himself able to shave in comfort for the first time in his experience while travelling at fifty miles an hour. And he was, of course, using the open 'cut-throat' type of razor that every man used in those days.

There were five coaches in all. The rear one was the *fourgon*, or baggage-wagon, which also carried the lavish kitchen and other necessary stores. Standing on its running-board was the *chef-de-train*, who sported a magnificent Vandyke style beard and a moustache so elaborately waxed that its points stuck out on either side of his face like twin darts. Next to the fourgon was Nagelmackers' triumph of a dining-car, half as long again as any coach any of the passengers had ever seen in their lives before. Through its wide and crystal-clear windows could be seen tables spread with snow-white cloths and napkins folded into intricate shapes of coronets and flying birds and butterflies. The gleaming cutlery and wine-glasses caught and reflected the brilliant light of the new-type Pintsch gas-lamps in the ceiling, each with no fewer than eight individual jets and fed by gas-cylinders slung beneath the coach between the bogies. On every table there were two cut-glass decanters filled with dark red Burgundy, and a vase of fresh flowers.

At the rear end of the dining-car could be seen the *plongeur*, a junior member of the kitchen staff, actually at work preparing vegetables for the meal that was to be served as soon as the Orient Express was signalled out of the station. But there was someone else aboard the dining-car, a man who was to achieve fame on this inaugural trip, a dominant personality almost to be compared with M. Georges Nagelmackers himself. M. About and his fellow-passengers caught a glimpse of him through a window as the train slowed to a standstill alongside them. He was the famous Wagons-Lits chef, a giant Burgundian with a black beard like a Scotsman's sporran and a pair of jet-black eyes that missed nothing. The Company well knew that a Frenchman expects to eat as well away from home as he does beneath his own roof; to ensure this, the Burgundian had been assigned the task of catering for them between Paris and Constantinople and back to Paris again on the return trip.

Next to the all-important dining-car came two sleeping-cars. Each of them, too, was half as long again as any hitherto seen on a railway track. Their windows were heavily curtained. Above them ran the splendid title: Compagnie Internationale des Wagons-Lits et des Grands Express Européens. It was the first time that the full title had been emblazoned on the Company's coaches. Separating the sleeping-cars from engine and tender was another fourgon. This carried the mail. Nagelmackers' Company had secured the monopoly of mail-carrying over the long-distance route, and the fee they received from the government was a useful subsidy to their enterprise, guaranteeing them a certain income which they could set off against the capital cost of building more and better sleepers and dining-cars as the years went by.

Train-spotters of today would be amused rather than impressed by the locomotive that headed this array of two fourgons, two sleeping-cars and a diner; but by the standards of the 1880s it was a powerful and up-to-date model. It was an 'Est' 2—4—0, with tall, flared, stove-pipe chimney, a brass steam-dome so highly polished that it glowed in the murky station air as though incandescent, and the customary paraphernalia of pipes and tubes and valves, control-rods, levers and linkage, exterior cylinders and brass-rimmed wheel-splashers. Its cab, of course, was open, with a roof so small that it hardly gave any shelter to the driver and fireman unless they stood close up against the firebox.

The passengers could hardly wait to scramble up the wooden steps lowered for their convenience by the conductors and explore the interior of this splendid train. Exchanging enthusiastic comments with one another, they climbed up and passed through the narrow doorways at each end of the coaches. They quickly deposited their hand-luggage in the compartments allotted to them, some of them two-berth, some three-berth, and one or two four-berth. Then, attracted by the appetising smell percolating through the cars from the far end, they made their way expectantly to the diner.

This car was Nagelmackers' pride and joy. Not for nothing was it entered in his Company's records as '*wagon-salon-restaurant*', 'dining-parlour-car', for it was in effect two coaches in one. To reach the dining-car portion it was necessary to pass first through a '*petit salon pour les dames*'. Adjacent to this was a snug little smoke-room for the gentlemen who preferred the comfort of easy-chairs to sitting over their cigars at table. This 'snug' could, if necessary, be cleared and fitted with tables to accommodate a greater number of diners.

Beyond this was the main portion of the dining-car. Tables laid for four occupied the whole of one side of the aisle; smaller tables, set for two, occupied the other side. All the chairs were upholstered in dark, embossed leather, with brass studs the size of doubloons close-set along the mahogany frames. These were not anchored to the floor but could be moved in and out from the tables to accommodate each diner individually, whether slim or stout. They stood on rich, dark-red carpeting, close-fitted so that no hint of draught could be felt around the diners' ankles.

The windows were spacious, seeming to fill the whole length of the car on each side. Every window had its own spring-loaded, pull-down curtain in addition to the hanging curtains of pleated damask, so that the diners could please themselves at each table as to whether they looked out at the flying landscape beyond the railway track or shut themselves in as though in their own snug home, within a little world, well lit and cosy yet travelling at forty, even fifty miles an hour, smoothly and almost without perceptible vibration.

The décor generally was characteristic of the age that had given it birth. By our mid-twentieth-century standards it was ornate and florid almost to the point of vulgarity. Hardly a square foot of the panelling in the end walls, the doors and the arched ceiling but had its lavish scrolls and curlicues, its swags of gilded flowers, its array of conventional and intricate geometrical designs. The ironwork of the brackets supporting the net racks that ran the full length of the car just above head level was a riot of contorted metal. The gas-lamps did their best to imitate the ornate crystal-and-gilt chandeliers of the Paris *salons*. Every detail, from door-knob to window-catch, seemed to have been made by a metal-worker seeking to outdo all that had gone before him.

As a result of all this there was an immediate impression of opulence, luxury and high-living that, the designers of the coach fondly believed, would appeal to the class of passenger for whom the Company expected to cater above all. Contemporary engravings show that it was the practice not only for the lady passengers but for the gentlemen too to retain their hats while eating their meals aboard these dining-cars: ornate, flowery hats, echoing the décor of the diner itself, were worn by the womenfolk; the men wore top hats or curly-brimmed bowlers, even when sharing tables with what they would doubtless have referred to as 'the fair sex'.

The train staff, of course, wore new uniforms to match the splendour of the coaches of which they were in charge. The man immediately responsible for the Orient Express, like his opposite numbers aboard the other long-distance sleeper-cum-dining-car trains that were to be brought into service, was known as the *Chef-de-Train.* He had, the Company's regulations stated emphatically, 'absolute authority'. Under his supervision, the personnel of the train consisted of one *Conducteur* (sometimes also referred to as *Contrôleur*) for each coach. On the Orient Express the conducteurs wore special armbands embroidered with the famous monogram 'O-E', of which they were inordinately proud. They wore peaked caps, with plenty of gold braid, piped jackets and trousers and highly polished boots. Waiters in the dining-car wore white gloves while serving the meals and pouring the wine.

In addition to the chef-de-train and the conducteur attached to each coach, the train carried three general handymen, and also one youth 'who shall be employed in manual tasks such as the handling of baggage and any other jobs that shall be allocated to him', as the regulations laid down. This lad probably 'doubled' as scullery-and-vegetable-boy in the kitchen, under the stern supervision of the all-important *Chef-de-Cuisine.*

The final portion of the dining-car, adjacent to the fourgon that carried the stores, was the kitchen. M. About was one of the passengers privileged to inspect it during the journey, and described it as 'but a hand's-breadth across'. It was a source of wonder to him that such excellent meals as they enjoyed throughout this inaugural trip could be prepared in quarters so cramped—especially since the giant Burgundian seemed to occupy every square foot of floor space with his huge bulk.

This man, it seems, made a great impression on all the passengers, and not merely on account of the superb meals he cooked in his diminutive kitchen. He was built on heroic lines, and possessed the temperament that is characteristic of men born in his part of France. He was flamboyant, emotional, highly excitable—as was to be noticed especially on the occasion when the Tzigane musicians boarded the Orient Express near the Rumanian frontier. M. About uses the epithet 'superb' more than once in describing him. But apart from a fleeting glimpse as the train backed into the station, the passengers saw nothing of him in the early stages. In any case, their prime concern was with the chef's handiwork rather than with the man himself. Now it was evening, and dinner-time. They were ready to eat.

1. M. Georges Nagelmackers, founder of the Orient Express

2. Mann 'Boudoir Car' of 1873:
Nagelmackers, on right, and Colonel Mann beside it

3. Interior of pre-Orient Express *Wagon-Lit*,
owned by Compagnie de l'Est (1875)

3

Hungarian Rhapsody

The station clock showed the hour. Prompt to the minute the chef-de-train blew his whistle, a flag was waved and, with a burst of steam and great churning of its coupled driving wheels, the 'Est' 2—4—0 began to haul its five coaches out of the Gare de l'Est on the first stage of the inaugural run of the new-born Orient Express.

The last glimpse of the station that the passengers caught, as they distributed themselves among the tables of the wide-windowed dining-car, was of the ancient sleeping-car that M. About had regarded with such distaste while awaiting the arrival of the luxury train. Was it a coincidence, he speculated as he sat down at his table with M. Oppen de Blowitz, that it had been placed within full view of this gathering of distinguished passengers now bound for Constantinople? Probably not, he decided: the astute M. Georges Nagelmackers had almost certainly placed it there deliberately, to point the contrast between the out-of-date and his own excitingly new wagons-lits! He chuckled with pleasure and amusement at the thought.

A quarter of an hour later the train was running smoothly out of the north-eastern suburbs of Paris into open country, into the wide continent of Europe, to the frontier with Asia beyond. The contented passengers, their first sensations of astonishment now subdued, unfolded their napkins and, as is the French habit still, tucked them into the top buttons of their waistcoats so that not a crumb of food or drop of wine should fall on to their clothes.

Though, like all his fellow-countrymen, M. About was a gastronome, and records that he preserved all the menu-cards placed on his table throughout the transcontinental journey out and back, he curiously does not give the menu for this inaugural dinner. But the dinner menus of the Orient Express service were always good, and this first one to be served on the train was probably better by far even than the one dated 6th December, 1884, when soup, buttered olives, fish with *sauce hollandaise*, lamb chops, chicken, buttered spinach, assorted fruit and assorted cheeses were served, together with the appropriate aperitifs, table wines, and liqueurs to follow.

M. About was loud in his praise of the Burgundian chef and his staff. Loud in his praise, too, of the refrigeration cabinets in the rear fourgon, which made it possible for the passengers to enjoy the butter of Normandy—in his opinion the best in the world—even when they were twelve hundred miles away in Rumania, on the far side of Europe. He strongly approved the Company's policy of putting on the tables the best wines produced in each country through which they passed. He noticed with pleasure that there were no fewer than four thin-stemmed wine-glasses beside each plate: a clear hint as to the variety they were going to be offered during the meal. But at the same time he had certain misgivings about this. Time and again in his peripatetic career he had seen good wine slopped on to the tablecloth, or down his own napkin, as a result of the vibration of the coaches in which he had been travelling.

But he very soon discovered that it was not just the skill of the waiters that enabled wine to be transferred from decanters to glasses without a drop being spilled; nor did he himself experience any difficulty in drinking from his glass. The dining-car was rock-steady even though, as he ascertained from the chef-de-train who came through the car to inquire of each passenger in turn whether everything was to his satisfaction, it was now travelling at little short of fifty miles an hour. It was with some pride that the official informed him that the dining-car, like the sleeping-cars, was fitted with the newly invented four-wheel bogies. This, coupled with superior springing, accounted for the smoothness of the ride. M. About, never a very good sleeper at the best of times, was enormously relieved to hear this.

The meal was long drawn out, as all good meals should be, and usually are when Frenchmen are eating. The passengers had been at table nearly three hours before the cognac was brought in. They had eaten course after course of delicious food; they had, as M. de Blowitz duly recorded, drunk 'wine red as rubies, white wine that gleamed as the topaz'. Champagne had been served, too. And not one of those slender-stemmed glasses had been seen to tilt and spill, even when the luxury train was rounding at speed the sharpest of bends in the track.

Good food and good wine established among the tables an atmosphere of good-fellowship that bathed the guests of the Wagons-Lits Company in a warm haze of shared pleasure. Glass in hand, they moved about, introducing themselves to one another, exchanging the names of mutual friends and acquaintances, establishing common interests. Cigars were well alight by now, and the dining-car was permeated with an aroma of rich Havana and the tang of excellent liqueurs. The contented diners were enveloped in it, linked to one another in the closest companionship.

It was nearly midnight when, as if by common consent, they left their embossed leather chairs to make their way from diner to sleeper. Some members of the party went straight to their compartments. Others, carrying with them their glasses, in which a drop or two of cognac still remained, lingered on the open-end platform of the car to savour the fresh night air as it rushed past them at nearly fifty miles an hour. These inter-coach platforms were to prove popular meeting-places for gossip and a smoke throughout the run.

Soon after half past five, by German time, the Orient Express pulled into the station at Strasbourg, three hundred miles from Paris. The station was remarkable for being among the first in Europe to be equipped with the then quite new electric lighting. M. Porges, President of the French Edison Company responsible for pioneering this, was extremely proud of what had been done, and even at this early hour was present with one or two of his closest associates to welcome the train and draw the attention of any interested passengers to the glories of the new installation.

Not surprisingly, there were not many of these at so early an hour after so late a night before: only some of the French railway company representatives who hoped to pick up a hint or two of value by inspecting the installation. M. About was certainly not among them, for all his keen interest in every aspect of the journey. He was still fast asleep when the train pulled into Strasbourg, and was still asleep when it was signalled away on its six-hour run eastwards to Vienna after a brief stop. 'They tell me', he recorded in his diary, 'that the lighting in the station was magnificent; but as for me, at that early hour of the morning the sun itself would have had little to commend it!'

He was much more concerned with the amenities of the train itself. He was a very fastidious traveller, and had suffered a good deal in the past from the conditions most travellers by rail had to endure. The sanitary arrangements, for instance. During his many years of travelling about the continent he had learned what hardships in this respect confronted the railway passenger. There were no corridors in the trains he had known. Passengers afflicted by what he tactfully refers to as 'the inescapable infirmities of human nature', after being cooped up for perhaps several hours at a time in a small compartment, had to snatch at their opportunity during the few minutes their train halted in a station. The railway companies, he had learned to his cost and embarrassment, did not bear the convenience of their fare-paying passengers in mind when arranging time-tables: stops at stations were rarely long enough.

Once again, though, he need not have worried in advance. He found the Orient Express toilets 'luxuriously appointed'. There was an ample supply of excellent soap. There was ample running water, both hot and cold. And hovering just out of sight, yet within easy hail at need, was a Company's servant who made it his business to clean the toilet between each passenger's use of it and the next. (This is something not met with on long-distance trains in this mid-twentieth century of ours.)

He had wakened at last to find that, beyond Strasbourg, the line had turned north, following the Rhine valley. The train was now skirting forest land, fertile fields, and the scattered vineyards of Württemberg. By lunch-time they had crossed into Bavaria. Through the windows of the diner they caught glimpses of the ruined fortress of Ulm, soaring above the waters of the Beautiful Blue Danube. It is not by any means always as blue as Strauss would have us believe. It was not blue when the Orient Express ran alongside it that day. M. About, a stickler for accuracy, called it 'filthy'. In German—the phrase he actually used—it sounds even worse: '*die schmutzige Donau*'. Soon afterwards river and railway-line parted company. The river swung north-east for Regensburg, the railway south-east for Augsburg and Munich. It was not, however, by any means the last time they were to see the Danube.

It was somewhere between Augsburg and Munich that the Orient Express had its only mishap of the trip: one of the bogies under the dining-car ran a hot axle-box. The stench of burning grease was soon in everyone's nostrils and everyone, even the least experienced traveller, knew instantly that something was amiss.

The news given to the passengers by the worried chef-de-train in person was not so much alarming as annoying. Repairs were necessary, and with the least possible delay. But they could not be carried out by the train crew. The train would have to reduce speed and make cautiously for Munich, headquarters of the Bavarian Lines of Communication over which they had now been running for several hours past. The diner to which they had become accustomed would have to be replaced by another before their eastward journey could be continued. There was no alternative to this decision. The chef-de-train deeply regretted that *Messieurs les Voyageurs* would be put to some slight inconvenience. Nevertheless, they must rest assured that the dining-car would be awaiting them, in perfect order, for their return trip from Constantinople.

Among the minor amusements of the party during this eastward journey was noting the discrepancies shown among the various station clocks. Paris time had been abandoned at Igney-Avricourt, to be replaced immediately over the frontier at Deutsch-Avricourt by German time. The two stations reveal the change of ownership: the Orient Express had now passed through Alsace-Lorraine into Germany proper. But at Muhlacker, twelve hours or so out of Paris, Stuttgart time replaced German time; and four hours later, while the dining-cars were being changed, Munich time took over. Three hours later still, strangely enough, Prague time replaced that of the Munich Hauptbahnhof clocks. This shifting about of time amused some of the passengers but irritated others, who could see nothing but confusion in it all.

Thirty hours after leaving Paris the train reached Vienna, nearly nine hundred miles, nearly halfway, along its journey. The train entered by the West Bahnhof, and clock-watchers noted that it was still 'Prague' time; they left Vienna by the Staats Bahnhof, where the time shown was that of Budapest! M. About had his usual comment to make, referring to the two clocks as registering 'Bohemian time and Magyar time'. De Blowitz rather irritably commented on the absurdity of this, especially in view of the fact that the train clock still registered Paris time. But his colleague had his retort ready:

> Evidently our dining-car clock has no intention of becoming embroiled in these Central European horological complications; it evinces a nice awareness of the wisdom of deliberate neutrality in the fact that it left its own key at home!

It was well after midnight when the Orient Express came to a standstill in the station in Vienna. Nevertheless very few of its passengers had gone to their beds. An air of expectancy permeated the train. There had been that rumour, on leaving Paris, that some Austrians, including some ladies, would be joining them. There was a good deal of speculation about this. Was it possible, a somewhat irreverent young newspaperman had asked out loud at table, that the Company was proposing to add to the good food, the choice wines, the excellent cigars, the luxury generally—the company of a few attractive young ladies to enliven their travelling hours? Might they perhaps hope . . . ? He had been shushed into an abashed silence by the rather austere M. Oppen de Blowitz, who, whatever he might secretly be thinking, did not feel that it was in good taste to start speculating openly about that typically French institution, *la p'tite amie*.

In fact, nothing so spectacular did take place. Awaiting the Orient Express on the main 'through' platform in the early hours of the morning was a small but distinguished group of travellers escorted by the station-master in full regalia, splendid as a soldier of the day in ceremonial uniform. Among them, as had been hoped, were two members of 'the fair sex'.

One of the party was Herr Wiener, no less a personage than the Secretary-General of The Imperial and Royal Austrian Eastern Railways Company. He was, of course, a man of some importance in his own right. Not many of the passengers, however, knew that he was own brother to the celebrated explorer whose exploits in the darkest and most dangerous reaches of the Amazon were at that time making the headlines in most of Europe's newspapers. With Herr Wiener were Herr von Scala, the Austrian Emperor's Minister of Roads and Communications, and Herr von Hollan and Herr von Obermayer, both of them State functionaries of some importance.

Imposing as these four men were, however, the passengers already aboard the Orient Express were more interested in the two ladies with the party now about to be conducted to the steps of the coach by the station-master himself. One proved to be Herr von Scala's wife; the other was his sister-in-law. Never mind, thought the travellers, their presence will introduce gaiety into the scene and afford them innumerable opportunities for displaying their native gallantry before their journey's end. They gave the immediate impression of being charming persons; their voices, M. About duly recorded, were 'as gracious as could possibly be imagined'.

It was late, and the party went straight to their beds. In the morning there were formal introductions and everybody was introduced to everybody else. M. About was greatly impressed with them:

Madame von Scala [he wrote] is most beautiful. She is somewhat of the English type, but more animated, with something of the Viennese about her which may account for this. Her sister, Mademoiselle Léonie Pohl, is exactly the opposite of what one thinks of as a classical beauty. But she is so intelligent, so charming, and has such a pretty wit, that she will certainly prove an admirable travelling companion. That may be seen at a glance. These two delightful sisters are enchanting to look at, with their profusion of ash-blond tresses, which would catch and hold the eye on any of our Paris boulevards were they to be seen there.

East of Vienna their route now lay over low ground, very much less interesting than the more mountainous landscape through which they had threaded their way after leaving Amstetten and Wels. It was a slow, rather tedious run of some six hours' duration by way of Bratislava and Nove Zamky, to rejoin the Danube as it ran through the twin cities of Buda and Pest. The first was the ancient, feudal city; the second was the industrial half. They were now 1,048 miles east of Paris.

A reception for the Orient Express had been laid on here: as much because of the importance of Herr von Scala's party as because this was the inaugural run of a new train. A band played lively Hungarian music that echoed and reverberated through the station, while formal compliments were exchanged among the representatives of the various railway companies travelling on the train. Then, because they had already lost some time through the mishap to the dining-car and had not made up all of it yet, the signal was given to board the train once more and it was flagged out of the station on the next stage of its run, a hundred miles and more to the far Hungarian-Rumanian frontier beyond Szeged.

It had first to cross a huge low-lying plain watered by the meandering Koros and Tisza rivers. It was a strangely empty plain: there were no towns, and even small villages were few and far between. M. About had crossed this plain once before, on one of his long, uncomfortable journeys. He had then been with a friend of his named Camillo, who later became a lay monk in Rome. They had been puzzled by the almost complete absence of any signs of human life and occupation. It was in the month of June and cornfields had stretched to the far horizons, ripening beneath the scorching summer sun; yet they had looked in vain for any sign of labourers, or even of labourers' cottages. It was strange to look out over this vast empty landscape. 'One would have supposed,' he said, 'that this extensive cultivation is performed by invisible genii!'

The only sign of movement in this area ten years ago had been the herds of high-spirited, apparently wild and ownerless horses, herds of cattle with terrifyingly long, curving horns, and buffalo ranging the plain at will. It was very different, he found, in 1883 as he looked out through the train windows. Now there were extensive orchards of fruit trees. There were acres of well-tilled soil with gangs of labourers hard at work on them. There were acres and acres of vineyards, all seemingly in excellent condition and bearing huge bunches of purple grapes. The busy little 'Est' 2—4—0 trundled its two fourgons, its wagon-salon-restaurant and its two wagons-lits across these limitless acres, stopping every now and then at stations, mere halts, often so small as to seem to have little reason for existing at all. But stop they did, for the policy of the Company was to lose no opportunity of drawing attention to this new and splendid railway service on offer to all who cared to avail themselves of it.

It was now early autumn. Grapes were being gathered in the vineyards. At each halt in turn, whether at the tiny nameless ones or at those which actually had a name on the map, such as Cegled, Nagykoros and Kecskemet, the passengers, already well dined and wined, were enthusiastically offered great bunches of Hungarian grapes—'delicious mouthfuls,' commented M. About, connoisseur and gastronome, 'if perhaps a shade too sweet for the taste of some of us.'

Maize was also being harvested. The landscape in the maize-growing districts was bright gold to the far horizon. Another picturesque feature was the display of pumpkins ripening in the sun: great sculptured vegetable boulders jutting out of the ground or ranged along stone walls and flat roofs to give them the appearance of weathered battlements. Dodging in and out of the entrances to these smallholdings, feeding in the lush grass of the river banks, were scores of white geese in magnificent condition. There were partridges in evidence, too. This was obviously the perfect terrain for them; these glorious game-birds would certainly flourish well here. The passengers watched some Magyar sportsmen—'two magnificently built men, tall and powerful, accompanied by two fine retrievers'—striding across the stubble of a field that had been newly harvested, their guns at the ready. They were barefooted, the soles of their feet obviously as tough as old boots! 'French sportsmen had better book passages aboard the Orient Express without delay, and stop off at one of these halts, where they could be sure of good partridge shooting. In France, poachers had ruined the sport for honest citizens!'

Memorable as these vineyards and acres of maize and white geese and whirring partridges were, however, these aspects of the great Hungarian plain faded into insignificance in comparison with their experience at the station of Szeged.

As the Orient Express slowed down alongside the low platform, a band of a dozen or so fantastically costumed Tzigane players who were standing on it raised their instruments and burst into wild Hungarian gipsy music so loud that it completely drowned the piercing blast of steam from the 'Est' 2—4—0's shining steam-dome. They played with an abandonment, a furious zest, that communicated itself instantly to the startled and delighted passengers. Ministers, high executives, journalists, publicists, even the two gracious Viennese ladies Madame von Scala and Mademoiselle Léonie Pohl, all crowded to the open ends of the cars, all dignity thrown to the winds, and scrambled pell-mell down the steps on to the platform to surround the players, pressing in upon them as though irresistibly drawn to their centre. M. About fell immediately beneath their spell:

> These astonishing artists [he wrote] played with a marvellous *brio*; they had the devil in their finger-tips and in their very bodies. They played not only their national tunes, the *czardas* of their race, but—in honour of the visitors from the West whom they were greeting so generously—tunes known and loved by us in distant France.

The violence of the wild Tzigane music was almost matched by the vigour of the applause from the staff and passengers who had by now all alighted from the train. It was impossible not to be carried away by the breath-taking rhapsodies, the sheer vitality of the players. Even M. Oppen de Blowitz, that dignified, rather aloof man, could not forbear to applaud heartily with the rest. He joined in every encore, but the players were not going to bother with mere encores: their repertoire was inexhaustible and they had a new tune in their heads and at their fingertips for every encore that was clamoured for.

But even the Orient Express on an inaugural run had a schedule to keep to, and long before the passengers had tired of the music the whistle blew a piercing blast and the conducteurs began urging their flock to come aboard the train once more. So this is the end of a magnificent occasion! was the thought in everybody's mind as, reluctantly, they climbed the wooden steps from the platform. 'Adieu, music and musicians!' M. About wrote dramatically. 'But stay! Why, the orchestra, to a man, has leapt aboard our train! They have crowded up the steps, and, lo, they have plunged like a wave into the wagon-restaurant!'

The arrival of the musicians created a sensation. But somehow, in retrospect at any rate, it all seemed an inevitable part of this epoch-making journey on the Magic Carpet to the Orient in which these passengers had been whipped off eastwards amid the glow of good living, good-fellowship, and the perpetual prospect of more and yet more good things still to come. As always, the train staff, from the chef-de-train and conducteurs to the youthful handyman, proved equal to the occasion. Tables were removed from the dining-car and stored temporarily in the fourgon. The chairs were placed close together round the sides. There was a general clearing of the decks. M. Edmond About takes up the tale once more:

And now, behold the younger members of our party seizing by the waist each in turn one or other of our charming female fellow-passengers and whirling them about the floor of our dining-car, until that moment the scene of so many memorable gastronomic occasions enjoyed in comparative quiet, while our fine musicians under their tireless leader, Onady Kahniar, played the most exhilarating of the Viennese waltzes! Now there was the devil not only in their fingers but in the twinkling feet of our dancing couples!

Viennese waltzes were interspersed with more of the national *czardas* and other wild Tzigane tunes. These filled the dining-car with sound until it seemed that ear-drums and side-walls alike must burst under the pressure. Tune seemed to beget tune; the circulation of the blood became more rapid as the circulation of the whirling dancers on the floor gained speed, whipped into a maelstrom of sound and movement by the tremendous vitality of the instrumentalists. And all the time, the Orient Express itself was gathering speed along the track, bound for the Hungarian–Rumanian frontier.

And the climax of it all had yet to come! When it did come it was sudden and wholly unexpected. Without warning the Tzigane players broke into *La Marseillaise*. The French as a race yield to none in patriotism: and here, in far Hungary, forty hours' travel from their native land, halfway to Asia, was their splendid and well-loved rallying-cry! Tears came into their eyes, and shivers of mingled pride and emotion ran up and down their backs: it was almost more than they could bear.

It proved quite overwhelming for the Burgundian chef, that spade-bearded giant whose culinary miracles had been a permanent talking-point throughout the journey. With the light of passion in his eyes he leapt at one bound from his cubby-hole of a kitchen into the centre of the dining-car floor. His tall white chef's hat practically touched the ornate ceiling. In one hand he waved a huge frying-pan, in the other was an egg-beater pressed emotionally to his barrel-like chest. In a stentorian voice that matched the full power of the combined instrumentalists he sang the French National Anthem at the top of his lungs, from first line to last, rising as he did so to a superb crescendo. It was an occasion no one present would ever forget.

But it came almost as suddenly to an end. As the train began to slow down on the outskirts of Temesvar (today's Timisoara), well beyond the frontier, Onady Kahniar and his eleven minstrels, after one last wild flourish of their music, slung their instruments over their shoulders and tumbled off the train as precipitately as they had boarded it nearly three glorious hours earlier. They grouped themselves on the platform for one last salute. M. Oppen de Blowitz contrived to engage their leader in conversation for a moment or two before the train left the station. When he asked him, would he and his men be returning to Szeged? Would it be on the next train? No, came the answer. Kahniar and his company had been engaged to play at a function in Temesvar that commenced in twenty minutes' time. They would be playing there for ten hours at least. Asked if they often played for so long at a stretch, Kahniar answered cheerfully that they had more than once played for fourteen hours and more, non-stop. 'We Tzigane players,' he ended, proudly, 'play just as you breathe. We get more tired *not* playing than playing, understand!'

4. Interior of pre-Orient Express *Wagon-Lit*.
Note absence of bogies

5. The Orient Express in 1883

HORAIRE DU GRAND EXPRESS D'ORIENT

Paris-Vienne-Constantinople

Station	Correspondance	Jours	Arrivée.	Départ.	Arrêts.
PARIS....	London, départ 10 mat.	Mardi et Vendredi		7.30 soir.	
La Ferté-s.-Jouarre	Calais, arrivée. 1.40		8.34 soir.	8.39 »	5
Epernay ...	Calais, départ. 2.16		9.42 »	9.47 »	5
Châlons-sur-Marne.	Châlons, arriv. 9.35		10.18 »	10.26 »	8
Bar-le-Duc..........			11.41 »	11.45 »	4
Toul..........		Mercredi et Samedi	12.51 mat.	12.54 mat.	3
Nancy..........			1.27 »	1.35 »	8
Lunéville..........			2.11 »	2.12 »	1
Igney-Avricourt..........			2.40 »	2.41 »	8
Deutsch-Avricourt..........			2.44 »	Heure allemande.	
				3.12 »	1
Sarrebourg..........			3.36 »	3.37 »	1
Saverne..........			4.09 »		
Strasbourg..........			5.02 »	5.07 »	5
Kehl..........			5.29 »		
Appenweier..........			5.42 »	5.47 »	5
Oos (Baden-Baden)..........			6.22 »	6.26 »	4
Carlsruhe..........			7 » »	7.05 »	5
Durlach..........			7.13 »	7.14 »	1
Pforzheim..........			7.48 »	7.50 »	2
Mühlacker..........			8.08 »	Heure de Stuttgard.	
				8.16 »	5
Stuttgart..........			9.18 »	9.23 »	5
Geislingen..........			10.44 »		
Ulm..........			11.30 »	Heure de Munich.	
				11.45 »	5
Augsbourg..........			1.24 soir.	1.27 soir.	3
München..........			2.35 »	2.40 »	5
Simbach..........			5 »	Heure de Prague.	
				5.16 »	5
Wels..........			7.04 »	7.10 »	6
Amstetten..........			8.45 »	8.49 »	4
Saint-Pölten..........			9.59 »	10.03 »	4
WIEN (West Bahnhof)......			11.15 »	11.25 »	10
WIEN (Staatsbahnhof)......				12.01 mat.	
Marchegg..........	hre de Prague	Jeudi et Dimanche	1.00 mat.	1.04 »	4
»	heure de Pest		1.18 »	1.22 »	4
Pressburg..........			1.54 »	1.57 »	3
Wartberg..........			2.27 »	2.31 »	4
Neuhäusel..........			3.47 »	3.51 »	4
Gross-Nana..........			4.38 »	4.42 »	4
Budapest..........			6.09 »	6.17 »	8
Czegred..........			7.56 »	8 » »	4
Felegyháza..........			9.13 »	9.17 »	4
Szegedin..........			10.31 »	10.36 »	5
Mokrin..........			11.29 »	11.33 »	4
Hatzfeld..........			12.14 soir.	12.17 soir.	3
Temesvar..........			1.06 »	1.14 »	8
Lugos..........			2.39 »	2.43 »	4
Karansebes..........			3.36 »	3.40 »	4
Porta-Orientalis..........			4.50 »	4.54 »	4
Herkulesbad..........			5.49 »	5.51 »	2
Orsowa..........			6.16 »	6.21 »	5
				Heure de Bucharest.	
Verciorova..........			6.30 »	7.45 »	37
Turn-Severin..........			8.07 »	8.09 »	2
Craiova..........			10.50 »	11 » »	10
Slatina..........			12.24 mat.	12.28 mat.	4
Pitesti..........		Vendredi et Lundi	2.18 »	2.23 »	5
Bukarest..........			4.45 »	5.15 »	30
Giurgevo (Smârda)..........			6.45 »		
Roustschouk..........				9.31 mat.	
Tchernavoda..........			10.09 mat.	10.14 »	5
Rasgrad..........			11.50 »	11.51 »	1
Ischiklar..........			12.31 soir.	12.32 soir.	1
Scheytandjik..........			1.12 »	1.30 »	18
Schoumla-Road..........			2.16 »	2.21 »	5
Pravady..........			3.09 »	3.10 »	1
Gubodjie..........			4.02 »	4.03 »	1
VARNA..........			4.31 »		
» (Lloyd Austro-Hongrois)				6.25 »	
CONSTANTINOPLE......		Samedi et Mardi.	6.00 mat.		

Constantinople-Vienne-Paris

Station	Correspondance	Jours	Arrivée.	Départ.	Arrêts.
CONSTANTINOPLE......		Jeudi et Dimanche		12.30 soir.	
VARNA..........		Vendredi et Lundi			
»				5.00 mat.	
Gubodjie..........			5.29	5.30 »	1
Pravadi..........			6.22 »	6.27 »	5
Schoumla-Road..........			7.15 »	7.20 »	5
Scheytandjik..........			8.18 »	8.30 »	12
Ischiklar..........			9.23 »	9.24 »	1
Rasgrad..........			9.58 »	9.59 »	1
Tchernavoda..........			10.20 »	11.25 »	5
Roustschouk..........			12.00 soir.		
				Heure de Bucharest.	
Giurgevo (Smârda)..........				1.30 soir.	
Bukarest..........			3 » »	3.15 »	15
Pitesti..........			5.29 »	5.34 »	5
Slatina..........			7.14 »	7.18 »	4
Craïova..........			8.35 »	8.43 »	8
Turn-Severin..........			11.21 »	11.23 »	2
				Heure de Pest.	
Verciorova..........			11.43 »	11.25 »	10
Orsowa..........			11.34 »	11.44 »	10
Herkules-Bad..........		Samedi et Mardi	12.09 mat.	12.11 mat.	2
Porta-Orientalis..........			1.12 »	1.16 »	4
Karansebes..........			2.13 »	2.17 »	4
Lugos..........			2.58 »	3.02 »	4
Temesvar..........			4.15 »	4.23 »	8
Hatzfeld..........					
Mokrin..........			5.38 »	5.43 »	5
Szegedin..........			6.28 »	6.33 »	5
Felegyháza..........			7.35 »	7.39 »	4
Czegled..........			8.37 »	8.41 »	4
Budapest..........			10.02 »	10.08 »	6
Gross-Nana..........			11.25 »	11.28 »	3
Kurth..........			11.50 »	11.54 »	4
Neuhäusel..........			12.14 soir.	12.17 soir.	3
Wartberg..........			1.20 »	1.23 »	3
Pressburg..........			1.49 »	1.50 »	1
Marchegg..........	heure de Pest		2.12 »	2.15 »	3
»	hre de Prague		1.54 »	1.57 »	3
WIEN (Staatsbahnof)......			2.47 »		
» (Westbahnhof)......			3.20 »	3.25 »	5
St-Pölten..........		Dimanche et Mercredi	4.40 »	4.44 »	4
Amstetten..........			5.54 »	5.58 »	4
Wels..........			7.33 »	7.39 »	6
				Heure de Munich.	
Simbach..........			9.30 »	9.24 »	5
München..........			11.44 »	11.49 »	5
Augsburg..........			12.57 mat.	1. » mat.	3
				Heure de Stuttgart.	
Ulm..........			2.39 »	2.34 »	5
Geislingen..........					
Stuttgart..........			4.35 »	4.40 »	5
				Heure de Carlsruhe.	
Mühlacker..........			5.44 »	5.45 »	4
Pforzheim..........			6.01 »	6.02 »	1
Durlach..........			6.37 »	6.38 »	1
Carlsruhe..........			6.46 »	6.52 »	6
Oos (Baden-Baden)..........			7.30 »	7.35 »	8
				Heure de Strasbourg.	
Appenweier..........			8.10 »	8.15 »	8
Kehl..........			8.30 »		
Strasbourg..........			8.48 »	8.53 »	5
Saverne..........			9.44 »		
Sarrebourg..........			10.19 »	10.20 »	1
				Heure française.	
Deutsch-Avricourt..........			10.43 »	10.21 »	
Igney-Avricourt..........			10.24 »	10.47 »	23
Lunéville..........			11.10 »	11.11 »	1
Nancy..........			11.47 »	11.55 »	8
Toul..........			12.30 soir.	12.33 soir.	3
Bar-le-Duc..........			1.40 »	1.44 »	4
Châlons-sur-Marne..........			2.53 »	3.01 »	8
Epernay..........			3.35 »	3.40 »	5
La Ferté-sous-Jouarre..........			4.48 »	4.52 »	4
PARIS..........			6. » »		

NOTA. — *Consulter l'Indicateur des Wagons-Lits, en cas de changement dans l'horaire du Grand Express d'Orient.*

6. A timetable for the Orient Express in 1883

4

Royal Reception

In the low-lying Tisa plain the countryside was emptier and more forlorn than any they had passed through since their long journey started. There was hardly a building in sight, and the few that were to be seen were tumbledown and poverty-stricken. Almost the only sign that man had ever passed that way was the track itself, over which the Orient Express ran cautiously, since the track might not have been designed to carry such an unaccustomed weight of rolling-stock. On the eastern boundary of the plain they were now close to the sprawling foothills of the Transilvanian Alps, a range of mountains that extended eastwards for two hundred and fifty miles in the direction of the Black Sea, and whose summits rose to more than 8,000 feet. For a railway-line, the only way was to turn south and pick up the valley of the Danube, which curves between the mountains to the north and the south, to break through the Iron Gate into the wider valley to the east that runs the whole way to the Black Sea itself.

The landscape became progressively more and more picturesque and impressive. But its impressiveness was linked with danger. Streams tumbled furiously off the foothills to join the Danube, and their swift passage undermined the railway track. The lower foothills were a mass of greyish-green marl, which has a tendency to swell when it becomes waterlogged and eventually to slide in great sheets which without warning could engulf and obliterate a track. In fact, only a week or so before the inaugural run there had been just such a landslide; a local train had been swept down into the bottom of the valley and totally wrecked, with heavy loss of life. This the passengers learned with some dismay when talking to a gang of permanent-way men working to reinforce a portion of the line over which the Orient Express had been flagged to a crawl.

At more than one point the passengers had their anxiety increased by the sight of long rows of men driving in massive piles intended to serve as a barricade in the event of another landslip. The fact that it was then autumn, with winter in the offing, did nothing to reassure them. It was something of a relief when darkness fell and curtains were drawn and the menace of a doubtful track could be forgotten in the warmth and comfort of the well-appointed dining-car. 'Out of sight, out of mind' was a comfortable saying, and more than one passenger sat back consoled by the reflection.

It was five o'clock on the Sunday morning when the gallant 'Est' 2—4—0 steamed into Bucharest station, more than fourteen hundred miles east of Paris, and came to a puffing halt. Its passengers were all still sound asleep. It had been decided that the halt at Bucharest should not be the customary five or ten minutes, or even the half-hour that was to become the normal length of the halt when the time-table for the regular Paris–Constantinople run was drawn up by the Est Compagnie. This first time it was to last a full twenty-four hours.

But certainly the passengers were not going to be left to their own devices for that long period. With the enthusiastic co-operation of M. Olanesco, Director of The Royal Rumanian Railways, over whose system the Orient Express was running for the last stages of its eastward journey, its passengers were to be taken on a four-hour trip by way of Ploesti, north of Bucharest, to Sinaia, in the very heart of those Transilvanian Alps they had been in full sight of for the past eighteen hours or so. Sinaia was located at a height of 2,000 feet above the Danube valley, below one of the 8,000-foot peaks that dominated the landscape for miles around.

At Sinaia, they were surprised to learn, King Carol of Rumania had recently built for himself, largely to his own designs, a summer retreat, the Peles Palace.

The expedition was organised with great efficiency. It was not necessary to change trains. The Orient Express was simply switched to the branch line that ran north from Bucharest to Ploesti and beyond, to its terminus in the mountains. As they approached Ploesti, M. de Blowitz noted with interest that oil-wells were being operated on a considerable scale. He noted, too, the presence of several troops of cavalry encamped in a large clearing among the trees. The tents were carefully aligned, the horses tethered in picket-lines, a number of officers and men were clearly enjoying off-duty hours, and 'the eternal female camp-followers prowled around the cavalry-lines'.

After Ploesti had been left behind the gradient steepened and the small train proceeded more slowly, winding among the foothills. On either side were precipices and ravines, above which towered 'frowning battlements of rock'. The passengers speculated as to how and where anyone might live, let alone build a summer palace, amid such menacing surroundings. Would there be, they wondered, a village at Sinaia? If so, it could surely be nothing more than a cluster of small hovels, every one of them permanently threatened by landslips in summer and autumn and avalanches in winter and spring.

How wrong they were! There were two rival hotels in this mountain resort so unexpectedly located at 2,000 feet above sea level. The party was entertained to lunch by M. Olanesco. Lunch was served in the open air, on the verandah of the Nouls Hotel, even though it was October. A Tzigane orchestra had been laid on by the management for their entertainment, and throughout the meal it played the same sort of wild Hungarian music they had first heard from Onady Kahniar's troup of instrumentalists. During their sumptuous meal, at which some notable wines were served, they were badgered at their tables by oriental carpet-sellers and by some peasant women who tried to persuade them to buy specimens of their native embroidery.

It was as they were leisurely sipping their coffee and cognac over their cigars that the bombshell dropped. An official from Peles Palace arrived in their midst and ceremoniously announced that His Majesty King Carol of Rumania would be pleased to welcome the entire company to a reception. This was a very special occasion: nothing less than the official inauguration of his new summer palace.

The whole company was seized with consternation. Not a man among them was wearing anything more formal than his usual travelling clothes. Certainly they were not suited to a state occasion. A spokesman on their behalf pointed this out to the palace official. The objection was courteously but firmly brushed aside: Their Majesties were well aware that they had made this long journey by rail without any thought of meeting Royalty; they would therefore be pleased to waive the customary etiquette.

Still somewhat embarrassed by the prospect, the party of travellers accepted his word and prepared to leave the hotel verandah for the Peles Palace, a mile and more higher up the mountainside. Their misgivings were increased when they walked into mist, which very soon turned into rain. The road degenerated into a track, better suited to mountain goats than to men, as M. de Blowitz bitterly commented. One or two of the party had umbrellas with them, but they offered little true shelter when the rain began to fall really hard. The track steepened, and narrowed. They were not wearing the sort of boots that such conditions called for, and very soon more than one of them had twisted an ankle, and all were becoming footsore.

Eventually they reached a remote monastery, which King Carol had used as his base when visiting the site of the summer palace he had designed. And now, though it was still a long way ahead of them, they could descry through the rain the palace.

High above our heads [M. About wrote] soared the silhouette at once elegant and bizarre of an edifice such as not one of us had ever seen except in dreams, or in books of fairy-stories when we were children. A chalet-palace in whose designing and building knowledge and fantasy had run riot together in timber, marble, glass, and precious metal.

The weary party were slightly encouraged when the strains of a military band were wafted to them on the breeze. The path, still narrow, brought them almost to the walls of the palace; and it was as they came to the palace gates that they all became most keenly aware of the pitiable spectacle that they must be presenting to the smart palace guards on duty there, and the palace officials waiting inside to greet them:

> Some of us in jackets, some in frock-coats, some with hard hats, others with soft; M. de Blowitz [About can rarely resist a crack at this oddly individualistic fellow-passenger] for some reason attired in the guise of a *Calabrian bandit.* Not one of us but would have given everything for the services of a valet, if only to brush the mud off our clothes and boots. We were as filthy as water-spaniels.

Despite what the palace official had told the party assembled on the verandah of the Nouls Hotel, about the waiving of etiquette, King Carol proved to be in full ceremonial dress when they were ushered into his presence. He received them with regal dignity, contriving to make each one of them feel, momentarily at least, that he was correctly attired for the occasion. They were shown over the palace, apartment by apartment. They were invited to admire the superb views from the great windows that looked out over the mountain slopes falling southwards into the valley far below. Finally, they were conducted to the Great Hall and bidden seat themselves to listen to a concert. This opened with a recital by a famous Rumanian operatic star, Carlotta Leria. The lovely queen herself, Carmen Sylva, accompanied the singer at the piano. After the concert they were given tea by the king and queen in person.

Not until dusk had begun to fall was the party permitted to take its leave. Each in turn was bidden a personal farewell by both Their Majesties. It was as they left that a ridiculous incident occurred. The party had been conducted to the Reception Room by way of the Great Staircase, at the foot of which they had deposited their dripping umbrellas, top-coats and hats. After their leave-taking they naturally made for the same staircase, to retrieve their belongings. Unfortunately they were mistaken by a palace official for workmen just leaving the premises. Firmly, and with a look of disdain that he made no attempt to conceal, the official led the party through a succession of corridors to a servants' staircase which deposited them in a small courtyard immediately beneath an overflowing gutter. 'It was raining still,' says M. About; 'raining as it only can in Brittany!'

The party were without umbrellas, hats and top-coats, and rapidly became drenched all over again by the water tumbling from that gutter overhead. Fortunately for them another palace official had realised what had happened to them and hurried after them to escort them back to the main staircase and a more dignified departure once they had collected their belongings.

Wet and chilled and uncomfortable and footsore, the party stumbled back down the mountain path, slithering and sliding about in the mud brought down by the heavy rain. From time to time they glanced back over their shoulders. The mountainside was now darkening as dusk fell, but on the higher slopes they saw that black had changed to white: the first snow of winter had just begun to fall.

What a relief that they were travelling in their own

train! The engine had steam up. They clambered hastily aboard the coaches and made for the warmth awaiting them. There was hot water in the basins, and they could wash and change into dry clothes. Their excellent conducteurs saw to it that coffee was brought to their individual compartments: good, steaming hot coffee that warmed them through and through. They towelled themselves briskly as the train gathered speed on the winding track that ran down from Sinaia to Ploesti and beyond.

It was ten o'clock in the evening, seventeen hours since their arrival in Bucharest. But their eventful day was by no means over. For now the whole party was to be entertained to dinner by General Falcoiano, Director-in-Chief of The Royal Rumanian Railways. His guest-of-honour at the dinner was to be none other than Colonel Candiano Popesco, His Majesty's senior aide-de-camp.

A fleet of cabs conveyed them from the station to Bucharest's best restaurant. Here they enjoyed sturgeon, some of them for the first time in their lives: a royal dish. They also sampled a dish of *sterlet*, which proved to be very young, or baby, sturgeon. That dedicated gastronome M. About was most enthusiastic about this, and admitted frankly that it was entirely new to him. 'May you be fortunate enough to taste this dish, if only once in your life,' he wrote; 'and served *au naturel*, as it was served to us, without garlic, without paprika, without any of those fierce condiments with which the Hungarian cuisine has the habit of poisoning such food under the pretext of improving it!' And M. de Blowitz wrote of the caviar that was served at this banquet that it was so superb that it made all the caviar he had ever tasted in his life before 'resemble nothing so much as black boot-polish'.

Wine flowed freely, a succession of liveried waiters refilling every glass as soon as its level began to fall. Notable among the wines was Imperial Tokay, from the other side of the frontier. Dozens of toasts were proposed, seconded, and responded to; during and after every toast, a glass of wine must be taken. It was well after midnight when the banquet came to an end and the passengers, many of them half asleep as a result of the mixture of mountain air and the fumes of strong wine, were returned to their sleeping-cars by the same fleet of cabs rattling over the cobbled streets of Bucharest in the small hours of the morning.

They all woke late. Woke to find that their train was now trundling southwards across yet another low-lying plain, having at last turned its back on the mighty Transilvanian Alps where they had been so royally entertained at the Peles Palace in Sinaia. Ahead of them ran the Danube. It was now a very much wider river than it had been when they first came to it, way back beneath the mighty castle that dominated the Bavarian town of Ulm. Had they known what it had in store for them not so very far hence they might have eaten their late breakfast of hot rolls and honey and strong coffee with a good deal less pleasure.

5

Last Lap

The frontier between Rumania and Bulgaria lay some fifty miles south of Bucharest. It was formed by the Danube, now a very wide, slow-flowing and turbid river that had still some three hundred meandering miles to go before it eventually flowed into the Black Sea. On the north bank of the river, still in Rumania, stands the town of Giurgiu, which in the pioneer days of the Orient Express was shown on the maps as Giurgevo. On the Bulgarian side of the river, immediately opposite, is the town of Ruse, which the passengers aboard that train would know as Roustschouk.

As the crow flies, from Roustschouk to Constantinople was some three hundred miles to the south-east. But there were two mountain ranges in between the river and their ultimate destination, so any route that might be practicable must wind a good deal in order to reach the other side of these mountains. Not one of the passengers had a map of the region; those who organised the inaugural run had been very reticent about the later stages of the journey since leaving Bucharest. One or two of the passengers—knowledgeable men like M. About and M. de Blowitz—had their suspicions that all was not going to work out quite as they had been led to expect. But they held their peace, sharing their apprehension with one another but saying nothing about it to the rest of their fellow-passengers.

The first hint they had that the remainder of their journey was not going to be quite as luxurious as it had been until that point was when, two hours' slow run from Bucharest, they ran into the outskirts of Giurgevo. It was a quarter past six in the morning. What then met their eyes appalled them. Giurgevo—today a thriving township of over thirty thousand inhabitants—appeared to be nothing more than a scatter of tumbledown buildings pretending to be a station. Here, they were told, they must alight and take the ferry across the Danube to the other side.

'But—the Orient Express?' someone asked, bewildered. 'How does that cross the river?'

'It does not. It remains here, in Giurgevo,' came the astonishing reply. 'We take another train on from Roustschouk.'

An appalled silence fell upon the passengers as the information sank in. They had understood from the first that they would remain aboard the luxurious train from start to finish, from Paris to Constantinople. Instead, it seemed . . . !

Already the train staff were off-loading their baggage. Urgently the chef-de-train indicated that the passengers would be wise to keep an eye on their belongings. The reason for his advice swiftly became apparent. For all at once a swarm of peasants in filthy and tattered fragments of clothing, barefooted and wild-eyed as savages, burst on to the platform like a pack of wolves and laid their grimy hands on every scrap of luggage they could find. Consternation spread among the passengers: were these thieves, determined to make off with their trunks and bags and bundles of warm rugs, their hat-boxes and other gear? The chef-de-train attempted to reassure them: these men were simply employed to carry the baggage from the train to the ferry by which the river had to be crossed. All the same, messieurs les voyageurs would perhaps be wise to attend each to his individual pieces of baggage.

For a while total confusion reigned. The raucous cries of these wild peasants filled the early-morning air. How different from the quiet and orderly progress they had enjoyed from one side of Europe to the other in the comfort of the dining-car and sleeping-cars! As they stumbled from the so-called station to the broken-down jetty, mud splashing over their boots and trousers, and mangy dogs sniffing viciously at their heels, they cast nostalgic glances back over their shoulders at the comfortable train that had been their home for so long past. Would they, the more timorous among them asked themselves, ever see the Orient Express again?

They had to watch their steps as they hastened along the broken-down jetty if they were not to rick their ankles in the gaps between the warped planks that were all that kept them from falling headlong into the turbid waters of the Danube below. It was a relief to step aboard the ferry-boat, which proved to be unexpectedly clean and ship-shape. Her captain welcomed them aboard in person, and wished each in turn '*bon voyage*' while in his care. Young stewards were ready to serve them immediately with cup after cup of strong, sweet, Turkish coffee—the first hint of The Orient they had met with.

They had one or two bad moments, though, during the

crossing. A number of enormous barges, which looked, as one of them remarked, like gigantic Noah's Arks, drifted aimlessly about the wide river, loaded down to the gunwales. Their tough skippers and swarthy crews obviously took pleasure in coming as near as they could to the ferry-boat, and indicating with loud cries and offensive gestures their intention of running it down. The passengers, alarmed at first, took comfort from the fact that their captain did not seem in the least perturbed, and exchanged rude words with the barge crews, giving as good as he got, while at the same time skilfully maintaining his course between Giurgevo and Roustschouk.

Half an hour after casting off from the Rumanian bank they were tying up on the Bulgarian bank. They stepped ashore on to a jetty as broken-down and hazardous as the one by which they had gone aboard. There was mud, and yet more mud. There was an air of primitiveness that was quite shocking even to the more experienced travellers among them. When they had gone aboard the ferry they had been sorry to leave behind them the comfort of the Orient Express; now, as they approached Roustschouk, they were already feeling sorry that they had had to say goodbye to the ferry. What awaited them in the next few hours they hardly dared to contemplate.

At the station there was a shock in store for them. The train, they were told, did not in fact go as far as Constantinople. There was not yet in existence a direct line to the Turkish capital. Instead, the train would take them to Varna, a small port on the Black Sea about one hundred and fifty miles to the east. It was a run of about seven hours—or, perhaps, a little longer, according to conditions.

'And then . . . ?' someone asked, tentatively.

'And then,' came the reply, polite but firm, 'we take ship for Constantinople.'

Horrified looks were exchanged among the passengers assembled on the platform to await the departure of the train. If Roustschouk looked like this, what sort of a place would Varna be? And what sort of a vessel plied between Varna and Constantinople?

The train was scheduled to leave at 9.30. No one was particularly anxious to go aboard. After the beautiful new coaches that had made up the Orient Express this was a sorry-looking outfit indeed. Nevertheless they had no option but to go; to be stranded in Roustschouk was unthinkable! With ill grace they took their seats, making the best of a bad job since there was nothing else they could do.

It was not a happy journey. To begin with the track had to climb to reach the plateau that extended to the south-east of Roustschouk. Then it ran fairly level for a few score miles. Then it descended gradually to sea level at the Black Sea port which was its terminus. It had been an expensive track to lay because of the varying difficulties of the terrain; it had cost something like 250,000 francs per kilometre to construct.

The track skirted innumerable forests, which, as the passengers peering through the small, dirty windows of their coach could see, had been decimated for their timber. There were long stretches of steppe country in which cultivation seemed to have been only very half-heartedly attempted, as though the labourers had no belief that anything would ever result from their efforts. Scattered about this desolate landscape were a few squalid hovels constructed of dried mud, timber, and rough thatch. They were isolated one from another, as though their occupants had no desire to maintain any contact with their neighbours. Small herds of cows and oxen wandered disconsolately about, with no herdsmen to tend them, not even an old woman or a child with a stick. The track was unprotected by any sort of fence, and time and again the train was brought to a standstill while the driver or fireman got out and went along the line to chivvy off some beast that was lying across it chewing the cud. Sometimes the beast would not move even then, and the engine was driven slowly forward until its cow-catcher succeeded in dislodging it from the track, and throwing it clear so that the train could proceed on its way once more.

It was learned that brigands roamed at large in this thinly populated region. Only a fortnight before, a gang numbering fifteen of these brigands had descended on the small station of Vetova. The station-master had been garrotted, and his small staff too. The station had then been stripped of everything that could be moved. The cash in the booking-office had been taken. A warehouse alongside the station had been pillaged. Then the station and warehouse alike had been set on fire. As the fire took hold, the brigands discovered the station-master's thirteen-year-old daughter, who had been hiding. They tied her up, and were about to throw her into the flames when they were interrupted by a gang of labourers approaching the station along the only road. At this, they dropped the girl and fled at full speed on their swift horses.

The general practice was to wait until the last train of the day in either direction had passed through (there were on average no more than two trains in each direction in every twenty-four hours), then descend in force, beat up the station staff and then proceed at their leisure to take what they wanted. An even worse crime committed regularly by these gangs was the stealing of lengths of railway line and sleepers. Quite recently, on this very stretch of line over which they were passing, no fewer than fifteen rails had been taken. The thieves were tracked down and apprehended; but so lax was the law in that part of Bulgaria, and so frightened were the authorities of the men involved, that they were let off without punishment. It was this constant pillaging of the single-line track that made progress so slow; for in the vast empty districts rails and sleepers could be removed even in daylight. The drivers and firemen had to keep constant and keen watch ahead lest the locomotives ran off the lines on to bare earth from which rails and sleepers had been removed since the last inspection. Information such as this did nothing to improve the ill-humour of the passengers now unhappily cooped up in this wretched substitute for the Orient Express.

At very few of the small stations was it possible to obtain anything to eat. But the train reached Scheytandjik just about lunch-time, and they had been informed that it would be possible to obtain something to eat there. M. About, always on the look-out for odd snippets of information, was amused to learn that the name of the station meant 'Little Devil'. He remembered this when he came to write about the so-called meal they had been offered there. Passengers' eyes had brightened when dishes of small partridge were placed before them. They looked most appetising. But: 'However sharp his knife, even the

Big Devil himself would not have been able to make any impression upon those innocent-looking partridges!' Wine was poured into their glasses, but proved on tasting to be 'unfit to offer to any devil, Little or Big'.

One and all, the disgruntled passengers pushed their plates away, rejected their glasses, and demanded something else. Eventually roast goose replaced the uneatable partridges, and this proved just possible to eat, 'dying of hunger as we all were at one-thirty in the afternoon'. Fortunately the goose was followed by a selection of rich Turkish pastries and then some stewed peaches 'garnished with almonds and drenched in a syrup which smelt and tasted of rose petals'. The unhappy travellers took heart once more: half their wretched trip to Varna at any rate now lay behind them.

They boarded the train for the second half of their journey to Varna. There was no improvement in the landscape generally. It was wasteland for mile after mile: vast empty plains, with the occasional bald hillock rising out of them to emphasise their monotony. There was an almost frightening element in the sheer emptiness and desolation; it was as if human beings shunned its very existence. And who could blame them? For a while there was not even any sign of water—the explanation, perhaps, of its entire lack of human habitation. Then one of the passengers spotted a trickle of a stream wandering vaguely down a shallow ravine as if it had no desire at all to be there. It ran into a stagnant-looking pool that seemed to be filled with hard, dead-seeming reeds that crackled harshly in the faint breeze like dry sticks catching fire. It lay alongside the track for something like ten miles: a gunmetal-grey expanse of dead water most depressing to look out upon from the grimy windows through which the despondent travellers continuously peered.

And so they came at last to the outskirts of Varna, on the western shore of the Black Sea. The immediate impression it gave was that it was as dead as the arid plain and the stagnant pool they had been looking at for many miles past. M. About and his fellow-passengers disembarked from the miserable train, in which they had been imprisoned almost without a break for more than seven hours, and headed for the quayside. The quay was a little more substantial than the jetties at Giurgevo and Roustschouk had been, but that was about all that could be said for it. As for Varna itself, they had no inclination whatsoever to go and explore it. 'A deadly hole of a place', M. About reported; 'the most inhospitable port in all Europe'.

Their troubles, though, were not yet over. They had yet to reach the Austrian-Lloyd vessel that was to convey them over the final stage of their long journey to Constantinople. But the water was not deep enough for the vessel to tie up at the quay. So, the hazards of small-boat transport from quay to ship awaited them. They were invited to descend the quay steps and pile into a number of wretched little row-boats, each manned by a villainous-looking Bulgarian with an enormous moustache and a fanatical gleam in the eye—own brothers, de Blowitz was convinced, to the brigands who made the nightly incursions on to the railway-line between Roustschouk and Varna and thought nothing of burning small girls alive in their bonfires.

The passengers were separated from their baggage, which was off-loaded into other small boats, manned by equally sinister-looking individuals. They looked untrustworthy in the extreme, and more than one of the passengers was convinced that he would never see his belongings again. What, they asked themselves, was to stop these evil-looking boatmen from turning back and making off with the baggage in their charge while the true owners were being rowed protestingly out to the vessel anchored off shore? These men were obviously in league with one another, probably all members of one large family and happy at the chance of doing a little banditry at the expense of these wealthy long-distance European travellers!

The unhappy passengers looked down at the black, oily water that flowed past the gunwales of the small boats in which they were so uncomfortably perched. They thought longingly of the comfort of their accommodation on the Orient Express. But at last they tied up against the side of the Austrian-Lloyd steamer awaiting them off shore. One by one they were helped out of the small fleet of row-boats and up the accommodation-ladder on to the deck. *Espero*, they were greatly relieved to find, was a much better craft than they had dared to expect. (Even her name seemed to them to indicate 'hope'.) She was clean and, as a ship should be even on the Black Sea and sailing from 'the most inhospitable port in all Europe', commodious and well appointed.

The passengers were welcomed aboard individually by the captain, as they had been at Giurgevo. They found that cabins had been reserved for them in advance—the best single- and twin-berth cabins in the ship. They had been warned in advance that though the Black Sea was an inland sea they must not suppose it to be nothing more than a lake. It was actually 168,000 square miles in extent, and could produce very rough conditions indeed, even quite close to the Bulgarian shore, which they would be following until they entered the Bosporus.

By no means all the passengers who joined the vessel at Varna were accustomed to sea voyages. It was a comfort to the more apprehensive among them that one of their number was Dr Harze, of Liège, a member of the Belgian delegation resident in Paris. He himself had travelled widely. He was a man of comforting presence, and had promised his fellow-travellers that he would guarantee their well-being throughout the trip. No one had felt any ill-effects on the long train journey, but not all were as optimistic about a sea voyage which, they were informed, would last all of fifteen hours.

Espero carried a very mixed cargo of passengers and merchandise. The majority of her passengers were poor peasant families on their way from Bulgaria to Turkey. These families, of course, could not afford the luxury of cabins, so they were distributed about the deck, and even in the holds among the cargo. From these holds, de Blowitz recorded:

> There arose into the evening air a smell of sweating humanity, of a whole population of men and women and children and babes-in-arms crowded together down there, jammed like sardines one against the other. They were facing the prospect of at least fourteen hours in the darkness and stench of the hold, worse housed than the flock of sheep which were packed in with our baggage and other merchandise in the after hold.

The Orient Express passengers had good reason to congratulate themselves on having the monopoly of the cabin accommodation aboard *Espero*.

The Bosporus, the narrow stretch of water separating Asia from Europe, is only nineteen miles in length, and is the gateway to Constantinople from the north, as the Sea of Marmara is the gateway from the south. An hour later, the passengers could see from the foredeck of the *Espero* the great domes of the centuries-old Mosque of St Sophia, the domes and minarets of the Mosque of Sultan Ahmet, and the towers of the glorious Topkapi Serai, soaring into the blue sky that hung over Europe and Asia alike. Excitement filled their breasts. The disappointments, hazards and discomforts they had undergone during the last stages of their long journey from Paris paled into insignificance in contrast with the sense of triumph they experienced in completing their journey, and the glories that were now displayed before them in this, the capital of the Ottoman Empire.

6

Return Trip

On Saturday, 13th October, nine days after setting out from Paris, the Orient Express party, having been shown the sights of Constantinople, made preparations to leave for home.

The trip back to Varna aboard *Espero* proved, however, to be as tranquil as the most apprehensive among the passengers could have wished. As the vessel cast off, they were still animatedly comparing notes about the extraordinary sight of the so-called Whirling Dervishes, whose religious rites they had been taken to witness in a monastery only that morning. It had been the high spot of an intensive round of sight-seeing. Constantinople had been filled with surprises for every one of them. They had shopped in the famous Kapali Carsi, the enormous bazaar which was almost a city within a city, with its streets of carpet-sellers, of coppersmiths, of jewellers, of tobacco-blenders, its dubious booths where the less adventurous-minded members of the party suspected unlawful transactions to be taking place behind heavy curtains, opium-pipes to be burning and, perhaps, razor-sharp knives to be flashing in the murky darkness. In the Turkish capital, even though it was then on the European side of the

Bosporus, they had experienced more than a whiff or two of the Mysterious East. The name of their train—even though, unhappily, it had not penetrated quite far enough—was aptly chosen: the Orient Express.

Now the Bosporus was as calm as a millpond. There was not a breath of wind. When darkness fell the moon shone from a sky crowded with stars bigger by far, it seemed to *Espero*'s passengers, than those to which they were accustomed in Western Europe. There were fewer passengers on this return trip than there had been on the outward trip from Varna, and they could wander about the deck unimpeded by scattered baggage and groups of poor peasants, their noses sniffing clean air instead of the pestilential stench they had to endure before. Some of the party, though tired after their days of continuous sightseeing, stayed on deck till well after midnight. A new passenger was making the return trip with them: a M. Georges Boyer, a writer of light verse who proved to possess a melodious voice and entertained them from time to time with bursts of song.

They left Constantinople soon after lunch. The majority went to their cabins soon after finishing their evening meal, just to be on the safe side, though the captain had assured them that the passage of the Black Sea from the northern entrance of the Bosporus as far as Varna would be a quiet one. But they had also been told that they would receive a somewhat early call in the morning; how early, none of them realised at the time.

Soon after three o'clock next morning *Espero* dropped anchor off the port of Varna. And as the anchor was dropped, the ship's two stewards set about waking the passengers. One by one they struggled into consciousness, looked at their watches through bleary eyes, and were staggered to find that it was not long past three o'clock. What, they demanded angrily, was all the hurry? Three-fifteen was no hour for a man to be fetched from his bed unless there was some sort of an emergency. The stewards were politely insistent, even urgent: *messieurs les voyageurs* must please hurry and prepare themselves to leave the ship.

But—why? The stewards did not explain. They spoke only a word or two of French, and few of the passengers talked the language of Bulgaria or Turkey. With a very ill grace they left their warm bunks and began to pull on their clothes. They could see a light or two on shore, and the black water surrounding the now motionless vessel caught a reflection here and there of her riding-lights. The moon and stars had disappeared; it was some hours short of dawn, a cheerless early morning indeed!

As they stumbled up on to deck, sleepy-eyed, irritable, chilled, some of them not more than half awake, they were greeted by the captain. He regretted the early call, but would explain the circumstances. Weather conditions over the Black Sea were unpredictable, and could be treacherous. A lifetime's experience had taught him that there were now signs of a storm blowing up. This had not been the case when they emerged from the Bosporus, but he had taken the advance precaution of warning his passengers that this sort of thing could happen; it had happened before. He had pressed his engine-room throughout the night in the hope that they could drop anchor off Varna before the advance-guard of the storm made itself felt. He regretted if his passengers had been inconvenienced by the undue vibration of his engine, but what he had done was in their interests, he could assure them. Meanwhile, since it was evident that a storm was approaching from the east, the usual quarter, the sooner his passengers were ashore the happier he would be—for their sakes, of course.

Now the row-boats were bumping and jostling *Espero*'s sides. Already the baggage was being lowered by the ship's crew into the larger boats on the starboard side. One by one the passengers scrambled down in the darkness into the smaller boats on the port side that were to ferry them ashore. It was a less tumultuous one than the outward trip had been, though the rowers continuously hailed one another just to make sure that all were heading in the right direction. When their shouting momentarily ceased, only the splash of their oars could be heard. One and all felt it to be an eerie trip, and longed for the moment when they could clamber out of the wretched row-boats on to dry—or even on to muddy—land once again.

Two men with flaring torches awaited them on the miserable Varna jetty. The passengers climbed up a rickety flight of steps and were seized, each in turn, by one or other of the men. Wretchedly, they stood in a cluster on the jetty, remembering the gaps in the warped planking that had made walking over them dangerous even in daylight. And even as they stood there, the first blast of wind from the east struck them.

It was only a minor blast to begin with: enough to make them draw their greatcoats a little more closely around them and move cautiously a step or two further away from the edge of the jetty. But the strength of the wind developed with uncanny speed, and before they had found their way off the jetty it was propelling them with uncomfortable rapidity in the direction of the station buildings. Now the surface of the sea was already being whipped into white-crested waves that would have lapped over the low gunwales of the row-boats in which they had been brought ashore. For escaping that, at least, they should be grateful.

Then, quite unexpectedly, their luck took a sudden change for the better. As they left the jetty and approached the station they were told that a meal had been laid on for them in spite of the early hour. 'A real banquet it proved to be,' M. About reported; 'a banquet to which I should have been glad to do real justice had my appetite been awake before my eyes had wakened!'

The party derived pleasure and amusement from watching a Bulgarian who had made the return journey with them and who had naturally assumed that the banquet had been laid on for his benefit also. Before their very eyes, M. About reported, 'this gentleman put away a plateful of cold game that had been intended for twenty people. It was a good thing so few of us at that hour were at all hungry!'

None of them looked forward with any pleasure to the return trip from Varna to Roustschouk, though they did realise that every quarter-hour put a few more miles between them and this 'deadly hole of a place'. After seven hours or so they arrived at Roustschouk, and stepped off the train, immensely relieved that no mishap had befallen them *en route*, no rails had been uprooted by those deadly bands of brigands about whom so many grim tales had been circulating. But on stepping out of the train they realised that the gale that had swept across the Black Sea from Russia had followed them, and even gone on before.

They could hardly maintain their balance on the platform; they staggered along the jetty to the boat, expecting every moment to be blown into the Danube; and the half-hour trip by ferry to the other side was an appalling experience, almost every member of the party being violently seasick from start to finish. Never had they been so glad to set foot on *terra firma* as they were when they left the angry waters of the wide Danube behind them.

Then, their eyes lit up, their spirits revived. For there, standing in the station of Giurgevo, was the Orient Express once more, the gallant little 'Est' 2—4—0 with steam up in readiness for the long haul westwards to Paris.

Their return trip was that of home-coming heroes. They were ceremonially greeted at every stop. At Bucharest a deputation awaited them which included Prince Bibesco. Great baskets of fresh fruit, peaches and grapes galore, were presented to them individually. At Budapest some of the party left the train for good. At Vienna some more of them, including Herr von Scala and his two ladies, who had proved such welcome additions to the original party that had set out from Paris, said goodbye.

They passed out of Austria on to German soil. By the Tuesday they were once again on French soil, soil so dear to M. About that there are tears in his eyes as he records his emotions on finding himself back in France. He catches a glimpse of a fold in the Vosges mountains in which his house was situated, the house from which he had felt obliged to exile himself when the Germans moved into Alsace, the house in which four of his children had been born. But it was his house and home no longer.

Now Paris was almost in sight. For most of the way west of Vienna the Orient Express had run at full speed. It had contrived to make up the two hours that had been lost somewhere east of Vienna. And, on the dot of six o'clock, the train slowed to a standstill in the Gare de l'Est from which it set forth—half a lifetime, it seemed to the less experienced of the passengers, before. Dusk was just beginning to fall. There were friends and relatives waiting to greet the 'heroes' of this great trek to the fringe of Asia and back again. There were officials too, of course, notably M. Moreau-Chalon, Vice-President of the Compagnie des Wagons-Lits et des grands Express Européens, who held his tall silk hat high above his head in a gesture at once of welcome and praise.

M. Grimpel, of the French Ministry of Finance, and therefore one of the most important members of the party that had travelled to Constantinople and back, asked how he and his companions could possibly show their appreciation of the magnificent hospitality they had enjoyed for the past fortnight and more.

It was—fittingly—M. Georges Nagelmackers who replied: he whose brain-child this had been, and who was responsible for the inaugural trip down to the last details. 'Why,' he replied, swift as a flash, 'the answer is simplicity itself. You will all come and have dinner with me tonight. It is already arranged!'

And so, on that happy note, the inaugural run of the Orient Express, Europe's first transcontinental train, came to an end.

7

Missing Link

If the passengers on that inaugural run of the Orient Express had been disappointed, even in some cases angered, by having had to do the last stage of the trans-European journey by boat, the Company itself was no less dissatisfied. From the start it had been its proud boast that passengers would be able to complete that run of almost two thousand miles without leaving the train; and this boast had not yet proved possible to make good.

The fault was not entirely that of the Company. The middle and late nineteenth century was a period of great expansion in Europe's railway system. Contemporary maps show an astonishingly elaborate network of tracks, not only through the larger countries, like the sprawling Austro-Hungarian Empire, but in the smaller ones too. Serbia and Bosnia, for example, which were later swallowed up by Yugoslavia, were establishing rail systems of their own; and the first of these was one on which the Company was keeping a very anxious watch. For it was through Serbia that the best possible overland route to Constantinople obviously lay: the route that would eliminate that change of train and final trip down the west coast of the Black Sea and the Bosporus.

These small countries had very real difficulties to face. They were poor, and they were often mountainous. The sprawling mountain ranges generally known as the Balkan Mountains placed almost insuperable obstacles in the path of railway engineers. An unbroken rail link between the capital of France and that of the Ottoman Empire, the Company realised, might take a long time to complete. Nevertheless they did not give up heart. They entered into long and complicated negotiations with the countries involved. Their aim was if possible to by-pass Bucharest altogether, to forget all about Giurgevo and Varna, to turn south instead of east and make use of a projected railway-line that would run from Budapest to Belgrade, then to Sofia, in Bulgaria, and so eastwards through Turkey-in-Europe to the capital. There was already a railway in Turkey for that final stretch; but it did not start till the far side of a Bulgarian mountain range that had not yet been mastered by the railway engineers. Until that mountain gap could be bridged, no through route was possible.

Two years after the inaugural run, however, much of the groundwork had been done. The Serbs and the Bulgarians had been persuaded that they stood to profit from the traffic that would pass over the new route. In 1885 permission was granted for the Orient Express to be re-routed. Certain trains would continue to run eastwards to Bucharest; but the true Paris–Constantinople route would be the new one. But there must be certain conditions. For example, from Belgrade onwards there was to be a limit of one hundred tons on the weight of the train in fair weather. If there was heavy snow, or if there were more than six degrees of frost, then one or more of the wagons-lits must be uncoupled and left behind; its unhappy passengers, even though they had paid the supplementary charge for the luxury of this special train, would have to do the best they could with a shake-down in the dining-car at night. If conditions really demanded it, the dining-car itself would have to be left behind.

The terminus of this new route was at Nisch (now Nis), some two hundred miles south of Belgrade and sixty miles short of the Bulgarian frontier. Anxious to attract custom, the Company issued an interesting brochure giving some details of this new route, rather as railway companies and travel agents today describe the country through which their customers will be travelling:

At 10.20 [the brochure ran] we leave Vienna for Belgrade. During the night it often happens that a storm breaks. Then is the time that the passenger is grateful for a snug compartment and a good bed! A mere touch on the bell beside his berth brings the attendant hurrying along the corridor outside, to take no matter what order he may choose to give. At 6.0 a.m. next morning we are passing through Budapest; soon afterwards we are once again making for the salon-restaurant to enjoy our breakfast. As we look out of our windows we take note of the harvesting and of the great herds of cattle and flocks of sheep, so numerous that at times they seem to blot out the vast extent of good pasture-land.

Now we run between the Tisa and the Danube, which we cross on a noble iron bridge at Pieterwaardein, after which we pass through a tunnel under the fortress. At 9.10 a.m. we reach the station of Maria Theresiopol [today's Subotica], where there is an excellent buffet at which they serve quite admirable wines in great variety. At last we come to Belgrade, 410 miles from Vienna, 1,250 miles from Paris.

From Belgrade to Nisch we pass through very pretty country, well cultivated; there are several fine bridges spanning the

Morava, and the stations are remarkably well kept. At Jagodin you should be careful not to miss a very beautiful mosque, in the Arab style, constructed in stone of divers colours—though nowadays you may be surprised to learn that the army is using it as a store for arms! We arrive at Nisch at 8.0 p.m. This is the second capital of Serbia, situated at 1,405 miles from Paris. Here will be found the Royal Residence, the Skoupchina.

The writer of the brochure had obviously made the journey in person, for he writes in much detail about the town. Passengers halting there will find, he tells them, that there are plenty of open spaces and streets attractively laid out. But that is by no means the whole picture of this 'second capital of Serbia':

Some of its streets are very roughly cobbled indeed, and you will find many of the poorer houses are built of sun-dried mud bricks, roofed with red tiles, and therefore a little primitive, though better than the corresponding ones to be found in Belgrade. Here, of course, live the working-classes. They work in agriculture, in the timber trade and the tanneries. When you leave the train you will board good carriages with excellent springs which compensate for the rough surfaces of the lesser roads. You will cross the Nischova, which flows through the town before entering the Morava. Your carriage will bring you to the Hotel de l'Europe, where you will eat very well for three francs, including all the wine you wish for; you may have a room there for only four francs. The beer brewed in Nisch is very good, and the wines are excellent and varied. We specially recommend to our passengers a Negotine, at two francs the bottle. (The local currency is the *dinar*, which corresponds roughly to the French franc.)

He has a good deal more to say about the amenities of Nisch. The little town is almost surrounded by mountains,

7. Interior of *Wagon-Restaurant* on the Orient Express in 1884

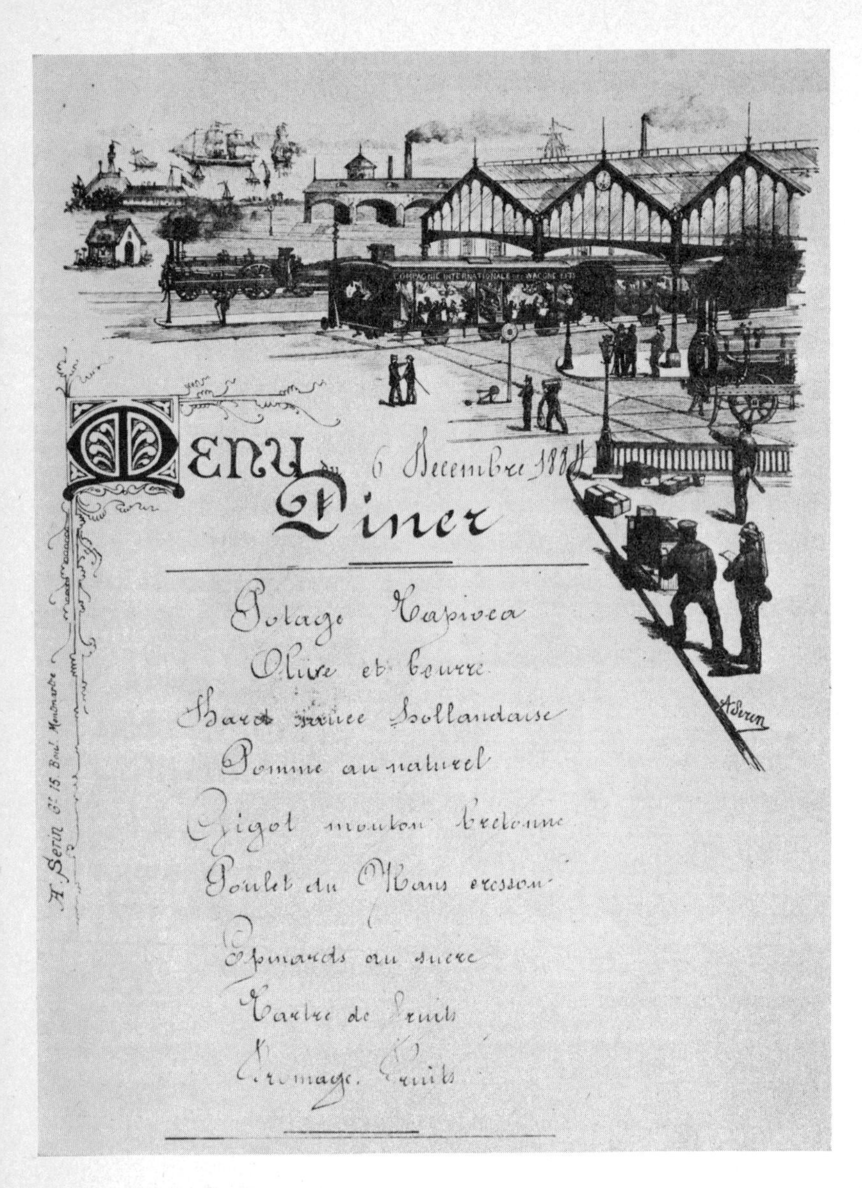
Menu du 6 Decembre 1884
Diner
Potage Tapioca
Olive et beurre
Bar sauce Hollandaise
Pomme au naturel
Gigot mouton bretonne
Poulet du Mans cresson
Epinards au sucre
Tartre de fruits
Fromage. Fruits

8. Orient Express restaurant tariff in 1884

and it is likely that some travellers may have felt strongly tempted to go no farther; for in fact, in 1885 and early 1886, Nisch was the end of the line. Travellers intending to go farther on had to leave the train and transfer themselves and their baggage to horse-drawn conveyances known as diligences. The next stage for them was a two-day—sometimes, in specially bad weather, three-day—trip over the mountains to the rail-head at the western end of the Turkish line at Tatar-Bazardjik. This was not a prospect that would appeal to every traveller; only the hard-bitten veterans would endure it.

One traveller who undertook this formidable journey south-east of Nisch by diligence made notes along the way which he later published for the enlightenment of other travellers who might be making the same journey after him. He was an observant individual with, obviously, a sense of humour. This was probably one of the most useful things to possess in those pioneer days of transcontinental travel. But you had certainly to possess in addition a toughness and resilience that is perhaps found today only in those who go out on safari, who penetrate the deserts and waste places of the world on foot or by Land Rover.

This traveller gave some details of the actual itinerary, and the timing. The stage from Nisch to Pirot, he wrote, began after a comfortable night's rest, though it involved a pretty early start. It was some forty-five miles to Pirot, but there was always a halt of some two to three hours at Bela Palanka, just midway through the stage. The diligences, he emphasised, were very comfortable indeed, and their excellent springing and upholstery would be appreciated by the travellers particularly on the rugged ascent of Mount Platcha.

Diligences were a form of stage-coach, rather smaller than those that plied on the English highways in the eighteenth century. They usually held no more than four passengers, their baggage being accommodated beneath the driver's seat and in the rear boot. They had a single shaft, with a horse on either side; one or more additional trace-horses were harnessed to it when the conditions of the terrain or weather demanded it. Though the actual compartment was small, with very small windows, and lightly constructed, the chassis was very solidly built to stand up to the strains imposed on the whole outfit on these long cross-country journeys.

The writer of these notes paid a good deal of attention to detail. He described the road as truly rural (which is not surprising in view of the fact that there were no towns of any size in the region), and 'full of interest'. The scenery was so beautiful and varied that the traveller would forget how much less comfortable he was than he had been aboard the Orient Express, and how much less rapidly he was being conveyed. Incidentally, he must remember to tell the driver of the diligence that he wished to make a stop at the inn to be found on the first shoulder of the mountain round which the road was curling. (Not, he adds, that the driver is likely to be annoyed at being requested to stop at any inn!) Only ten yards from the inn, two fine springs are to be seen gushing out of the rock.

Neither driver nor passengers, however, will choose to drink from these springs, for the innkeeper makes use of the crystal-clear water 'in the brewing of a herbal concoction from a recipe known only to himself, which many knowledgeable travellers have already found to be of benefit to their health. One glass of this infusion,' he declares, 'will put you into good heart for the long descent on the farther side of the mountain which now awaits you.' And he adds, for the comfort of the nervous passengers, that the downward gradients are much less severe than those that led up to the pass, and the taste of the herbal concoction will still be in their mouths when, four hours after leaving Nisch, the diligence arrives at Bela Palanka, midway along the stage to Pirot.

Bela Palanka means 'White Fortress'. It was a large village lying at the foot of a slope descending from twin hills known as the Big and the Little Courilo, foothills of the higher Sua-Planina Mountains an hour's travelling-time away. Our expert traveller makes it clear that there is nothing worth buying in its few shops, but there is one good hotel, the Hotel de l'Europe, where Italian is spoken as well as Serbian and Bulgarian and, of course, French. He strongly recommends the exhausted passenger to make straight for the amenities of that hotel when he has alighted, cramped and stiff from the diligence.

From Bela Palanka to Pirot is a stage of some five hours. The last part of the journey, he warns his readers, is deceptive: they will see their destination while they are still a very long way away from it, for it lies in the middle of a plain, surrounded by mountains, and for something like two tedious hours the diligence will be leisurely descending the winding road down the northern chain of the Passara Mountains.

And when at length you arrive, what is there to see in Pirot? It possesses one main street, along both sides of which, when he was last there, houses were being built. Otherwise it is just the 'Old Town': a 'rabbit-warren of alleys and Turkish-style hovels in an indescribable state of dilapidation. The Nischova flows through it, and from one of the timber bridges spanning it a painter,' he says, 'would find enough that is picturesque to occupy him for a long time.' Probably the most notable landmark, in fact, is the old Turkish fortress, now falling into ruins, towering above the Hotel Roi de Serbia, where the weary traveller can engage a room for a franc and a half and eat and drink his fill for a couple of francs more.

Mr A.T. (as he invariably referred to himself) was not the only person to write about this new stretch of territory through which the railway was eventually going to run. The Company, too, issued a brochure which covered the stage beyond Nisch. It was compiled a year later than Mr A.T.'s notes, when there had already been some developments. A few more miles of track had been laid, and more yet were in prospect. The Company was very anxious to keep prospective passengers up to date with these developments.

We anxiously await the day [said the brochure] when the complete Orient Express train will be able to continue the full distance beyond Belgrade. Meanwhile, we have recently provided a wagon-lits of ten berths to establish a temporary service beyond Belgrade and Nisch to Bela Palanka. This vehicle will run at least as far as Pirot next October; this will reduce from three days to two the journey that now has to be made by diligence to rejoin the railway at Tatar-Bazardjik, the western end of the line owned by the Ottomans. This vehicle will certainly make the journey more comfortable and pleasant; furthermore, it will enable the passenger to sleep in his own berth at Nisch, and thus spare him the trouble and expense of seeking a hotel room. He will find an excellent meal available for him at the station buffet. The following morning the same vehicle will carry him, in two hours or so, to Bela Palanka, some thirty miles from Nisch.

The writer of the Company's brochure, like the travel agents of today, went to some trouble to interest potential customers in the country through which their route lay. He dug out fragments of history and legend and slipped these in among the more factual portions of his text, so that passengers had something interesting to read before and during their long journey through unknown territory. He told them, for instance, about the famous 'Tower of Skulls', which was to be found close to the Military Hospital two miles beyond Nisch and close to the new railway-line. The sinister name derived from an episode which took place some sixty years earlier, during the war between Turkey and Serbia.

A small contingent of riflemen, determined to throw off the Turkish yoke, was forced by superior numbers to retreat up the mountainside to this fortress. There, for a long time and against ever-increasing numbers, the gallant little band held out, barricading themselves inside the fortress and determined never to yield. Their food ran short and the spring inside the fortress ran dry; their powder and shot ran dangerously low. Soon it became clear that it could only be a matter of hours before they would have to give in to their enemies who were closing in upon them from all sides.

Then [says the brochure] the Serbian officer in charge had an inspiration. He commanded that all firing should cease. He collected from every man the last of the gunpowder he possessed, and with this he 'mined' the fortress. Then, with a show of surrender, he lured the Turks to the fortress and opened the gate to them. The moment they had poured in, the gate was slammed shut behind them and the gunpowder store was fired. The explosion killed almost every one of the Turks, and the Serbs to a man. The Turks who survived cut off the heads of the dead men, Turks and Serbs alike, and with them built the tower that is still to be seen, close to the railway-line.

It was a grisly story, rather oddly calculated, perhaps, to 'enliven' the journey of passengers on the Orient Express over this new section of the route. In fact there were only a few more miles of line to carry this small wagon-lits. It ran through the defile of the Nischova, skirting the flanks of Mount Platcha (which only the previous year had had to be negotiated by diligences on what were little more than mountain tracks). There were a number of redoubts to be seen in the region, built by the Serbs at various commanding points after the disastrous Battle of Pirot. It was savage country: a mass of precipitous heights from which boulders were likely to fall at any time, threatening passengers whether by road or by rail. And it ended at Bela Palanka, 'White Fortress', rather more than halfway to Pirot, which, by the following year, the Company hoped passengers would be able to reach in the comfort of their wagons-lits. But this would not be, unhappily, just yet.

For the time being it would be necessary to transfer once more to the diligences. Now the route would pass mainly through wheat and maize fields spread out at the foot of small hills. At Pirot it would be possible to buy carpets woven locally in brilliant colours. There would be opportunity to make such purchases, for the horses must be given at least an hour's rest. There was, passengers were told, one quite good inn, bearing the somewhat pretentious name, Hotel Nationale. The food there was good, and the charges were reasonable.

Twelve miles beyond Pirot lay the Bulgarian frontier, at Tzaribrod, which was no more than a small village. And beyond Tzaribrod lay the notorious Dragoman Defile, which winds through close-set gorges, arid and savage and, at that time, overlooked by menacing fortifications.

Mr A.T. in his useful notes has something to say about this new stretch of country, south-east of Pirot. He does not think much of Tzaribrod, where meals were of very poor quality. But he is enthusiastic about the route on the other side of the frontier, where 'the road plunges into the first of a succession of mountain gorges, at first perhaps a little forbidding but always notable for their dramatic quality'.

After a while the diligence comes to a halt in a small village named Slivnitza. The Company's brochure ignores this, but Mr A.T. has a good deal to say about it, with undertones of warning to the unsuspecting traveller:

> Slivnitza is only a small village, the first house on the left of which is an inn. The proprietor, a M. Calche, will offer you paprika, eggs, wine and Turkish coffee—dull sounding fare, perhaps, though in the circumstances in which you now find yourself it will seem sumptuous indeed. The circumstances, as a matter of fact, are such as you will find difficulty in wholly ignoring: hard wooden benches to sit on, a floor of beaten earth beneath your feet, carcasses of sheep with their throats cut hanging about you from beams overhead, fishing-nets here and there, smelling of stale fish; and—above all else—hordes of flies which with the best will in the world you are unlikely to be able to ignore!

Fortunately for travellers obliged to break their journey in Slivnitza the stop was a very brief one. The horses had to be fed and watered, but as the city of Sofia was only two hours' travel away the drivers were always anxious to get on as soon as possible. A plateau had to be climbed, and from this could be descried the domes and cupolas of Sofia's many churches shining clearly in the sun against the backcloth of the 7,000-foot mountains beyond. The horses could smell their stables, the drivers their lodgings and friends; the diligences rattled briskly over the rough roads and their passengers forgot their discomfort in their thoughts of what awaited them in the Bulgarian capital, a city of some twenty thousand inhabitants in those days.

There, says Mr A.T., the wise traveller will have reserved rooms for himself in advance at the best hotel—and he names it: Hotel de Bulgarie. There still remain some sixty miles or more to the rail-head where the Turkish train to Constantinople will be boarded. The horses will require twenty-four hours' rest; the drivers and passengers alike will be in need of rest and refreshment before the final stage of this gruelling journey. Being something of a connoisseur in food, the excellent Mr A.T. recommends the discerning traveller not to take all his meals at the hotel but to seek out a restaurant run by a Frenchman, M. Lazare, where French cooking at its finest will be met with. The restaurant is easy enough to find, for it is right opposite the Bulgarian Finance Ministry's buildings, a useful landmark.

There were still sixty miles to go before the rail-head was reached. Halfway, there was a break at Ikhtiman. Diligence passengers would be more than ready to alight in the village, for the road from Sofia was little more than a track, with loose boulders on it that were capable of overturning a vehicle if the driver was not alert to avoid them. The track wound about on the slopes of a series of hills; now and then there might be a cluster of hovels too small to merit the name of village, for the most part, though at two of them, Novihan and Vacarel, it might be possible to obtain light refreshment. More encouraging, though, than any refreshment were the signs at the second of these two villages that there really would be—some day—an extension of the railway: labourers were already at work clearing a route along which the track would eventually be laid.

Some idea of the condition of the mountain road can be gained from the fact that even the most expertly driven diligences took something like six hours to cover the thirty-odd miles from Sofia to the midway staging-point, Ikhtiman. Nevertheless, Mr A.T. feels it is as well to warn the intending traveller of what awaits him there:

> Ikhtiman is the least comfortable of all the halting-places you have encountered so far. It is a *wholly wretched* sort of a place, a muddle of unpaved or ill-paved alleyways, narrow and tortuous beyond belief. Nevertheless, here you must be willing to linger for some two hours while your horses are fed and watered and rested, to enable them to gather strength for the trek over the mountains that faces them immediately they leave the outskirts of Ikhtiman.

Though the water may be fit for horses to drink, he adds, human beings will do well to avoid it, and to drink the rough wine of the district instead: it is less lethal than the water! But certainly the traveller must fortify himself in advance, for the last thirty miles of the final stage are if anything worse than those that have just been completed. The gradients are steep, the surface of the track rough, rocky and uneven. The horses have the utmost difficulty in maintaining even a mere walking pace, and often that pace drops to a mere crawl. It is not unusual for harness to break, even for a wheel to be shaken off the axle. Passengers will be shaken in the diligence like butter in a churn—and there is nothing whatsoever that they can do about it—save grin and bear it. Probably they will not even notice the superb scenery that is displayed on either side of them as they travel eastwards. But they should try at any rate to look out of the windows as the diligence reaches the summit, for the view down the mountainside is magnificent: a great circle of mountains, with a beautiful valley at their base—in the centre of which lies the longed-for rail-head of Tatar-Bazardjik.

He was absolutely right in his praise of the magnificent spectacle offered to the weary traveller over this last stage of his interminable journey. The Stara Planina range runs eastwards from Sofia, curving roughly in line with the Rumanian-Bulgarian frontier; they merge with another range, the Rhodope Mountains, fifty or sixty miles to the south and running approximately along Bulgaria's southern frontier with Greece and Yugoslavia. Some of their summits rise to between 7,000 and 8,000 feet. It was beneath their northern foothills that the Turks had built their own railway-line eastwards from Tatar-Bazardjik to the Turco-Bulgarian frontier and to Constantinople beyond. This was the line which those unhappy travellers by diligence were so anxious to reach, so that they could complete their two-thousand-mile journey in the relative comfort of a train.

The approach to Tatar-Bazardjik, however, was not wholly attractive, according to the writer of the Company's brochure, anxious as always to be honest as well as informative:

We begin the descent of the eastern slope of the mountains, making now for the village of Vitreana. This wears something of the air of a necropolis, all its houses being closed and shuttered. But soon we are at Tatar-Bazardjik, where rooms await us at the Hotel Macedonia. Here we sleep, to rise in the morning in time to catch the single daily train, which leaves for Constantinople at 6.30 a.m.

Mr A.T., however, recommends travellers to put up at the Hotel Djianik, because it is considerably nearer the railway station than the Macedonia. He does not think any better of Tatar-Bazardjik than the Company's brochure-writer does. Between them they paint a pretty gloomy picture of this rail-head. It is, they agree, a derelict sort of a place, made up of Jews, Roumelians, Bulgarians and Turks. While the railway was being built it did come to some sort of life; but once the construction work was completed, the place began to die on its feet. 'You will not be sorry to leave it,' says Mr A.T. 'It contains nothing of interest for the traveller—not even a single monument—and its numerous minarets and towers are rapidly falling into ruin.'

Dismal as it was, it was at least a place where the bruised and battered travellers-by-diligence could rest and recuperate a little. They had nearly twelve hours there. No one explained to them why it should be that the one train of the day to Constantinople had to leave so early in the morning: how they must have wished for the opportunity to lie in bed just a little longer before getting up and making for the station!

So, now once again the traveller was on board a train; there were no more mountain roads to be negotiated. For the remaining four hundred miles or so his journey would lie through easy valleys and over relatively low-lying plains. Now it was possible to keep to a rigid time-table; the passenger would in future know just where he was at any given hour. The Company's brochure set it all out clearly for him in a final page or two, to ease his mind and encourage him:

> Having left Tatar-Bazardjik promptly at 6.30, we arrive in Philippopolis [today's Plovdiv] one hour later. We are now some 1665 miles from our starting-point, Paris. We are struck by the fact that the people are in general livelier, more gracious, and better looking than those of the countries we passed through as we skirted the right bank of the Danube. Now we follow a route to Adrianople [today's Edirne], along the valley of the Maritza. At 11.25 we stop at Tirnova-Semenly, and there partake of a more than adequate meal, for which we pay two francs. And less than two hours later we arrive in Moustapha-Pacha, the frontier with Turkey. One hour later we pull in to Adrianople, 1750 miles from Paris. We have averaged twenty-six miles an hour over this section of our journey!

And so the itinerary continues, with stopping-places, brief descriptions of the landscape, and a mention of the manœuvres of the Turkish cavalry which may often be watched on the wide plains of western Turkey. The writer of the brochure drops a hint from time to time that travellers have doubtless noted the difference in the standard of comfort between that of the Orient Express on which they started their long journey and the Turkish train they have to use for the final stage. He does this in a sly fashion. For instance he says that after six hours of travel 'which the luxurious coaches supplied by the Company might have made endurable' the traveller will arrive at Tcherkesskeuy (also called Tcherkeuy). But now he may feel cheered, for at this station there is a Hungarian restaurant whose fare will do much to restore the downcast and exhausted passenger.

Will this interminable journey ever come to an end? Yes, indeed it will! At two minutes to four the train pulls in to Tchataldja, one of the foremost landward defence-points of the Turkish capital. On its walls and towers the passengers will be able to pick out sentries silhouetted against the pure blue of the oriental sky. Next, the train is running alongside the lake of Sparta-Koulé. Just beyond lies the Sea of Marmara, on which may be descried vessels bound for Constantinople, their white sails sharp against the background of the mountains of Asia. At 6.40 the train passes through the great westward wall that protects the city. At seven o'clock it comes to a halt at last. The passengers alight, to find themselves in the Old Seraglio, only a few steps from the Mosque of St Sophia, their journey of more than two thousand miles at last at an end.

The writer of the Company's brochure had striven manfully to persuade would-be travellers that there would be compensations for the rigours of the two- or three-day stage of the journey by diligence, and the final stage in the slow Turkish train between Tatar-Bazardjik and the capital. But he also voiced his Company's longing for the day when the entire journey could be completed in the luxury of the rolling-stock M. Georges Nagelmackers had designed and built for the Orient Express, to be run and maintained by the Est Compagnie of Paris.

In fact, that day was not far distant. Working against tremendous odds, and in the face of appalling natural hazards—the mountains with their raging torrents, the tumbling boulders, the extreme cold, the violent winds, the weeks of ever-deepening snow—the railway engineers eventually linked Nisch with the existing Turkish rail-head at Tatar-Bazardjik.

There came the day, the first day of June, 1889, when passengers could entrain at the Gare de l'Est, Paris, stake their claims on their individual and cosy berths, their places at table in the sumptuous wagon-salon-restaurant, and not leave the train unless they wished to do so until, just sixty-seven hours, thirty-five minutes later, the Orient Express came to a halt in the terminal station at Constantinople, capital of the Ottoman Empire. The overland route of the Orient Express was at long last a reality; an engineer-visionary's dream had at last come true.

8

Royal Passengers . . .

The Orient Express was now firmly established as the first great trans-European railway service. Travellers in every country were made aware of it by clever publicity devices —the forerunners of the advertising methods used so widely today for every conceivable 'commodity', whether package-tours or packaged detergent and toothpaste.

Among the most persuasive of the forms of advertisement in the middle eighties of last century were the two books written by those unusual men M. Edmond About and M. Oppen de Blowitz: *De Pontoise à Constantinople* and *Une Course à Constantinople*. Both were published within a year of that famous inaugural run. It is true that neither had written with any enthusiasm about the final stage of their journey, by Austrian-Lloyd boat from Varna to the capital. But the Compagnie Internationale's publicity men soon had new brochures in circulation, emphasising the improvements in the service that either had taken place or might be expected at any time. Every enterprising traveller was keen to sample the thrills of a two-thousand-mile trans-European rail journey, if only to be able to boast about his experiences to his stay-at-home friends on his return.

The heyday of this travel, with the Orient Express as the 'King' of long-distance trains, was between the years 1890 and 1914: twenty-four years during which the passenger-lists kept by the chefs-de-train and the conducteurs, and later preserved in the Company's archives, seem to contain the names of practically every individual who had become a personality—either because of fame or because of notoriety.

Kings and queens, reigning or abdicating, princes and princesses, travelling openly in state or incognito; ambassadors, ministers of state, diplomats; millionaires, absconding financiers and runaway confidence-tricksters operating on the grand scale; spies and smugglers—of diamonds, gold or dope; internationally known figures like the Aga Khan, members of the Rothschild family, deposed monarchs of relatively little-known states in the days when Europe was divided up into far smaller portions than she is today; oriental potentates, Indian maharajahs with their vast entourages: all these, and innumerable others availed themselves of the luxury and comfort, the safety and speed, the discreet service of the Orient Express as they shuttled to and fro across Europe.

Some of the chefs-de-train and the conducteurs kept diaries and notebooks of their years of service to the Company, towards which they felt an almost fanatical loyalty. The contents of these notebooks and journals make fascinating reading today, and throw a brilliant light on an aspect of fairly recent history that is not to be found in the history textbooks. Turning these pages, you repeatedly come across snippets of information and comment that are revealing, sometimes dramatic, often amusing, always rewarding in one way or another; and

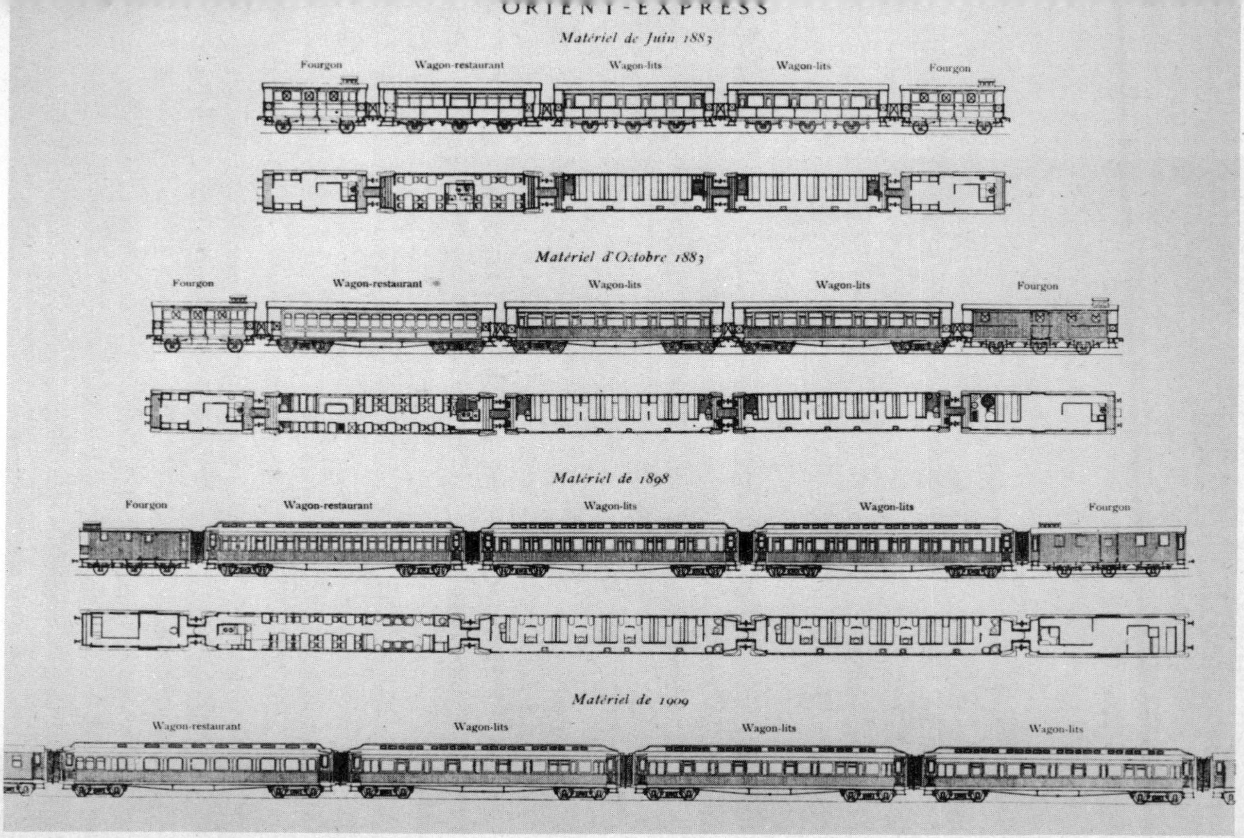

ORIENT-EXPRESS

Matériel de Juin 1883

Fourgon
Wagon-restaurant
Wagon-lits
Wagon-lits
Fourgon

Matériel d'Octobre 1883

Fourgon
Wagon-restaurant
Wagon-lits
Wagon-lits
Fourgon

Matériel de 1898

Fourgon
Wagon-restaurant
Wagon-lits
Wagon-lits
Fourgon

Matériel de 1909

Wagon-restaurant
Wagon-lits
Wagon-lits
Wagon-lits

9. Make-up of Orient Express trains 1883–1909

10. Interior of a 'Special' Orient Express as laid on for the President and other such dignitaries

11. One of the C.I.W.L. first restaurant cars fitted with bogies (1883)

all have the merit of having been recorded at the time; they bear the stamp of immediacy and truth.

One of these writers of memoirs was a retired chef-de-train who in his years of retirement set up as a restaurant-proprietor on a site overlooking the track on which his beloved Orient Express had regularly run while he served on it, and was running still. He claimed to have 'rubbed shoulders from 1900 to 1914 with the greater part of the Crowned Heads of Central Europe'. At seventy-three years of age he was still hale and hearty, and among his greatest pleasures was to sit on the terrace of his restaurant with a crony, or even a new customer, and, glass in hand, tell stories of the good old days when he was an internationally known employee of La Compagnie. Like other writers of these memoirs, he emphasised the importance of absolute discretion at all times:

One must *see* nothing, *hear* nothing [he used to repeat]. Nevertheless, that did not mean that we did not *possess* both eyes and ears! But—we were the soul of discretion. We *had* to be.

However, there was an episode which, strangely enough, involved a case of *lèse-majesté*—and you know what that can mean! It was, I think, in the year 1904. King Ferdinand of Bulgaria was travelling on my train with his young son Boris, then only ten years old, who later succeeded to his father's throne. The boy and his father occupied the special compartment, of which all the curtains were kept firmly drawn. It was impressed upon me that no one must be allowed to peer into the compartment, or even to linger in its vicinity. And on no account was the young prince to be allowed to draw the curtains aside and look out into the corridor. 'During my absence in the dining-car, or elsewhere,' His Majesty said to me, 'it will be your responsibility to see that my instructions are implicitly obeyed.'

But it was not to be as easy as all that, as the chef-de-train was to find out. On one of his rounds he found himself almost nose to nose with young Prince Boris, who had drawn back the curtain and lowered the window to see what was going on in the corridor. He shook his finger warningly at the small royal passenger, and the curtain was promptly dropped. But on his very next round he saw the royal nose pressed hard against the window of his compartment. He was thus faced, as he says, with an 'agonising decision: His Majesty's instructions had, of course, to be obeyed to the letter; it was as much as my job was worth to ignore them. On the other hand—how could I carry them out without risking very real trouble?'

He was indeed in a quandary, but there was not a moment to be lost in coming to a decision: it was to be either disobedience or—*lèse-majesté*! But it was for his character that he had been appointed chef-de-train: his qualitities of discipline and decision. He would exercise them right away, and take the consequences, whatever they might turn out to be.

He removed from one foot the soft leather slipper he ordinarily wore when making his night rounds in order to avoid disturbing light sleepers. Then, swiftly and silently, he reached round the door and 'applied the slipper briskly to the young prince's posterior. And that did the trick!' On his subsequent rounds the curtain remained firmly closed. Nothing was ever said to him about the incident. He often wondered whether young Prince Boris told his father what had happened. But whether he did or not, the king continued to regard him with favour. In fact, not long afterwards he bestowed upon him one of his country's decorations, one which, as he proudly declared, he 'would not dispose of even if it was the only way of obtaining food and drink to fend off starvation!'

King Ferdinand of Bulgaria was a monarch who had an absolute passion for train travel and used the slightest excuse for a journey westwards from his capital, Sofia, through Austro-Hungary, Germany and France. His son proved to have inherited his father's enthusiasm. Conducteurs and chefs-de-train had innumerable stories to tell about him. They recall being aboard the Orient Express on more than one occasion when Boris insisted on travelling, not in the special royal coach but—on the footplate! He had made it his business to learn the technique of engine driving, and when the mood was upon him would insist on taking over the controls.

One day, a conducteur has placed on record, the train came to an unexpected and unscheduled halt, just beyond Vienna. He looked out to see what the matter was, and to his surprise saw a man hurrying alongside the track beside the stationary train and then climb nimbly up the steps into the cab of the engine. There was no doubt whatsoever as to his identity: he was, of course, King Boris of Bulgaria!

The train started off almost at once, and it seemed to the conducteur that it was travelling at a considerably greater speed than was customary over that particular length of line. The driver told him later that King Boris had ordered the fireman to stoke the furnace to its maximum capacity, so that an immense head of steam would be generated. He himself had been alarmed at the speed at which the king, who had snatched the controls from him, was driving the train. The Company's regulations were always to slow down a little just before any of the long curving portions of the line where it followed the curves of the river; but with the king at the controls the train seemed to be going faster than ever at those points. Even worse, he was taking a perverse pleasure in slamming on the brakes hard, and without the customary warning whistle.

Not surprisingly, the ordinary passengers aboard the Orient Express complained bitterly of the discomfort, and even danger, that they experienced on such occasions, and the Company was forced to take a firm, if diplomatic, line: there must be no further interference with the driving of the train, a task which had been delegated to experts who were professionals, not just gifted and erratic amateurs.

But Boris, determined not to surrender, was equal to the challenge. In future he bided his time until the Orient Express had crossed the frontier and was running over tracks laid in his own country. Having sat impatiently in his special compartment until the frontier was crossed, he took action. He pulled the communication-cord and, before the train had quite come to a standstill, descended to the track, ran briskly along it and climbed into the cab to take over the controls at last. He was now, so to speak, on his 'home ground', and lord of all he surveyed. And surely, he would have argued if the point had been raised, among what he surveyed was the Orient Express itself, which he had every right to halt in its tracks on his own side of the frontier, if he wished to do so. And—he did!

On the last occasion when he played this trick the circumstances could have been calamitous. While he was on the footplate there was an explosion when a steam-pipe cracked. The official driver was badly scalded by the blast of high-pressure steam. Boris, who had fortunately been looking out over the side of the cab at the time, escaped injury. He took over the controls and brought the train to a standstill so that the badly injured driver could receive medical attention from the first-aid equipment always carried in the fourgon. He then drove the train on to the nearest station, where an ambulance was waiting to take the patient to hospital. Pressure was brought to bear upon him by his government, after that episode, and he wisely acceded to their insistance that he should give up driving engines, whether on his own lengths of track or in other countries.

King Boris's death remains a mystery to this day. No one knows just how it came about, halfway through the Second World War. The Company firmly believes that he died violently at the hands of the hated Gestapo. He is remembered by chefs-de-train and conducteurs alike with affection as well as with respect. Though he could cause them infinite bother, and test their self-control to the limit, and had done so ever since, as a ten-year-old, he had worried that chef-de-train, he appeared to them an endearing character, one who shared their own enthusiasm for the crack train which was their mobile home for most of their lives and to which they were fanatically devoted.

There were other kings who used the Orient Express: Léopold II of Belgium, for instance, who had been king for twenty years already when the train made its famous inaugural run. He travelled frequently on the train, usually, for reasons of his own, incognito; and very often in the company of the world-famous dancer, Cléo de Mérode. In fact, so frequently was the special coach booked in their name that among themselves the conducteurs used to refer to 'Their Majesties Cléopold'!

Another European monarch well known to the train

staff was King Carol II of Rumania, great-nephew of the King Carol who had entertained the party making the inaugural trip when he invited them to visit his new palace at Sinaia. This king was a little more discreet in his movements than the Belgian king was; his travelling companion was a certain Madame Magda Lupescu, for whom he at one time renounced his throne. Later he ascended the throne again. Madame Lupescu was not much liked by the staff on the Orient Express, and was known—well out of earshot, of course!—as 'the pudgy Pompadour'.

More colourful by far than any of these, however, and a monarch in his own way, was the famous Maharajah of Rana Bahadour. No one who ever met him could ever forget him, and the tales told about him by the conducteurs and chefs-de-train on the Orient Express are legion. He travelled always with an immense entourage. And he tended to travel, also, as one of the chefs-de-train recorded, 'with seven of his wives in a state of barely concealed nudity'. Such startling goings-on could have their comic and near-tragic aspect, as one particular incident makes plain.

On that particular occasion the Orient Express included a privately chartered wagon-lits together with a privately chartered wagon-salon-restaurant: these were for the exclusive use of the maharajah and his party. Their hire cost a small fortune; but the maharajah had a large fortune, and to him the expense was so slight as to be imperceptible.

His party boarded the Orient Express by way of a platform railed off from the other passengers using the Gare de l'Est, and from the curious sightseers too. Only when they had all gone aboard were the two special coaches coupled up to a light engine and hauled out of the station and back down the platform from which the train would be leaving in a quarter of an hour's time. The light engine was uncoupled and left the station. No sooner had it done so than the main train was backed in as usual. Then the special coaches were coupled up, behind the rear fourgon, in readiness for the two-thousand-mile run to Constantinople, where the party would take ship for India.

From start to finish the curtains in the windows of the special coaches were kept closely drawn. Two conducteurs, specially selected for their known discretion and long experience, mounted guard on top of the steps to ensure that no inquisitive newspaperman, or anyone else, managed to intrude.

But though the curtains were drawn throughout the run, rumours began to spread among the remainder of the passengers before many miles had been covered. It was understood that a whole salon-car had been converted at the dictates of the maharajah. The armchairs—considered fully adequate for ordinary travellers, however distinguished they might be—were replaced, so it was said, by divans upholstered in swansdown and covered with silk and damask and cloth-of-gold in the most exotic designs and the richest imaginable hues. They were heaped with swansdown-filled, silk-covered cushions to accommodate the weight of the self-indulgent Indian and his harem of seven wives. Heavy curtains hung at the entrances to the two special coaches, which in any case were isolated from the rest of the train by the massive stores fourgon which ordinarily formed the last coach of the train.

It was no business of the train staff whether the maharajah's religion permitted him one or a dozen wives, though the chef-de-train and the conducteurs concerned could not help feeling a little shocked the first time they encountered the party. This had been at Constantinople, where the party had entrained for a journey to Paris, the journey which they were now preparing to do in reverse. But if they were a little shocked, they kept their feelings to themselves: they were the servants of the Company, and their first duty was not to their conscience but to the Company and its customers, whether occidental or oriental.

Imagination, however, ran riot among the passengers generally. Remembering stories they had read of the ways of oriental potentates whose religion permitted them any number of wives and concubines, they remembered, too, the illustrations in those books: the veiled and amply proportioned beauties whose fleshy charms were so inadequately concealed by the trousered robes they wore of the most diaphanous silk. What a time the maharajah and his party must be having, back there in the luxuriously appointed special coaches!

Maybe they were. But when the unforeseen occurred, they were the passengers who suffered most. This was the episode talked of for long among the Orient Express staff. They may have felt amusement; they may also have felt a slightly puritanical sense of complacency as they looked back upon it.

Towards the end of the eastward run, somewhere along the line beyond Philippopolis, in that valley between two Bulgarian mountain ranges that they had to thread before the landscape opened out as they approached the Turkish frontier, the heating system in the special coaches broke down. It was then winter. A furious gale from the north-east was sweeping across the Black Sea and into Bulgaria from Russia. It carried in its teeth snow that carpeted a landscape and mountainscape already iron-hard after several months of unbroken frost. There could not have been a worse time for the heating to break down, for the train was now running in open country where stations were few and far between; and at none of them, even if the train had been stopped, would there have been mechanics capable of effecting the sort of repairs involved.

In those days one of the most important items of baggage any traveller carried with him was the 'hold-all': a pair of sturdy straps into which were rolled a number of thick, woolly rugs. They were a stand-by, a survival from the days of travel by stage-coach when the only means of keeping out the cold of winter was to wrap oneself up in a cocoon of rugs and try to forget the weather conditions until the end of the day, when the traveller could thaw out in front of a huge log fire and drink a steaming hot toddy. With a long greatcoat of the type fashionable at the turn of the century, often more like a huge cloak with an all-enveloping cape attached, and with one or more rugs wrapped snugly round his shoulders and feet, a man could keep warm in almost arctic conditions.

But the Maharajah of Rana Bahadour and his seven wives were not accustomed to that tradition of travel. By comparison with the Europeans, they were 'travelling light'. For them it was not a question of heavy tweeds, mufflers and greatcoats but of rare silks, in the case of the womenfolk light as gossamer. They were immediately affected by the breakdown of the heating and the cold that at once began to pervade their coaches; and they were the least well equipped of all passengers to cope with the situation.

The maharajah summoned the conducteur responsible for their comfort and well-being, and explained the situation. The conducteur accepted it; but he pointed out that as a result of this extreme cold all the coaches were experiencing the same trouble, in greater or lesser degree. Pipes were freezing up in all of them. Courteously, the maharajah said that he was sure that this was so; but, speaking now with a certain firmness, he made it clear that he considered that he and his party were entitled to special consideration. Something must be done—and at once—to ensure that the heating was restored in his special coaches, whatever might be done about the rest of the train.

The conducteur, like the chef-de-train who had been faced with the alternatives of disobedience or *lèse-majesté* towards King Ferdinand, was faced with a dilemma. He was personally responsible for the well-being of the maharajah and his party; but he was also a servant of the Company, who had always laid it down that all customers must be treated with equal respect and consideration, and that partiality must never be shown if it was to be at the expense of someone else.

If he was to show partiality towards the maharajah it could only be at the expense of the remainder of the passengers; if, somehow, extra heat was to be obtained for the occupants of these special coaches at the rear of the train, it could only mean that the other passengers would have to be sacrificed. To his credit he refused to agree to the maharajah's very emphatic request for preferential treatment.

'But we *must* have warmth,' the unhappy husband of

seven wives insisted. 'If we cannot have our heating back, then you must obtain for us some warm garments.' And because the conducteur looked taken aback at the request, he called for his aide-de-camp and took from him the purse he always carried with him. Gold coins such as the conducteur had never seen before were poured out of the purse, first into the maharajah's hand and then into that of the astonished conducteur. 'Go and obtain for us such warm garments as you can lay your hands on,' he said urgently. And he added through teeth that were just beginning to chatter: 'Please be as quick as you can!'

The conducteur departed, and sought the advice of the chef-de-train, the man who, he knew, always had an answer to every problem. The two of them conferred. And within half an hour they had returned to the special wagon-salon at the rear of the train with the most extraordinary assortment of clothing. There were blankets and tasselled tartan rugs, a railwayman's greatcoat or two, mufflers and rough jerseys and other garments, collected from the train staff and the few passengers to whom a gold coin or two was ample reward for feeling the cold rather more than usual.

Rapidly the maharajah's personal servant sorted the random selection of clothes and rugs and distributed them on his master's behalf among the lightly, seductively clad wives, each of whom, in accordance with native custom, had a tiny diamond set in her right ear-lobe and another in her right nostril. Valuable diamonds, of course; but without the power to warm the wearer!

Gravely the chef-de-train and conducteur stood by and watched. If (as is almost certain) they were amused by what they witnessed, they were far too discreet to permit the ghost of a flicker of a smile to appear on their lips. And the maharajah himself retained his dignity throughout, though nothing like this had ever happened to him before. He and his party, he realised, were now clothed in a hotch-potch of garments that made them look, in comparison with the gorgeous attire that was customary among them, like the beggars whom their guards and their dogs would chase away from the palace gates if ever they attempted to approach so near!

Another conducteur has particularly good reason to remember a member of European Royalty who more than once travelled on his train and who, rather surprisingly, could at times prove more than a little 'difficult'. *Mauvais* is the word he used of him in his memoirs; but the word does not mean exactly what it is said to mean in French vocabulary-books. It means not so much 'bad' as, perhaps, unpredictable. This particular member of a more than ordinarily distinguished Royal Family, the conducteur said, had a habit of seizing on some whim, particularly in connection with food, and then insisting on indulging it whatever the difficulties he might cause. He would insist on being treated, aboard the Orient Express, exactly as if he were at home in his father's royal palace, where all the resources of the spacious kitchens were at his disposal. On one of these journeys, says the conducteur, he rang the bell and told me that he had a fancy for a dish of mackerel *à la Capitaine Cook*. 'Naturally I told him that the entire cuisine was at his service. Then I went along to see the chef-de-cuisine. The chef protested that he had no mackerel in his store-cupboards; and even if he had the mackerel, he had never heard of them being served *à la Capitaine Cook*. Nor, as it happened, had I!'

The conducteur was in a quandary. He knew better than to return to the royal suite and tell its occupant that there were no mackerel on board the train, and that anyway the chef had never heard of this particular fashion of preparing and serving them. So, at the first stop he asked the station-master to telephone down the line to Vienna to ask that mackerel should be obtained and be brought to the station to meet the train. He also asked the station-master to make inquiries as to this particular method of serving the fish in question.

In due course the Orient Express drew into Vienna's Hauptbahnhof. The station-master there was quivering with anger. Did the conducteur suppose, he asked in a strangled voice, that it was possible to go shopping for fish at three o'clock in the morning so as to have a crate of mackerel waiting for a train that halted for a few minutes at four o'clock? This might be the practice in France, where everybody made a god of his stomach, he said with a sneer on his lips. Doubtless French housewives went shopping by candlelight; but all good Viennese, the conducteur might be sure, were well and truly asleep in their beds at such an hour!

Of course the station-master was quite right. But it was not he who would have to go and break the news to this exacting royal customer that there would be no mackerel *à la Capitaine Cook* on his table that day; it was the unhappy conducteur who would have to perform this task. And as he duly recorded: This prince was so angry at the failure of the Company to indulge his foolish whim that, at journey's end, 'not so much as a sou did he give to any one of the staff of the train!'

9

. . . and Others

It was not necessary to be Royalty to rate an entry in the notebooks, diaries and memoirs of these chefs-de-train and conducteurs. There were the eccentrics, too.

There was the Austrian countess who travelled several times every year to Paris for the sole purpose of having her beloved miniature poodles trimmed there. She was so particular about everything that she brought her own personal maid with her, and the maid used to strip off the bedclothes of her mistress's bunk every night and make it up again with a clean pair of exquisite black silk sheets fragrant with perfume from the great store-cupboards of the *schloss* in the mountains of Austria which was her home. She ate the food supplied and served from the Orient Express kitchen, but her poodles had to be fed with special food which she brought with her and handed personally to the chef with detailed instructions as to how it was to be prepared. She fed her pets herself, and the conducteur firmly maintains that their diet was every bit as delectable as her own.

It seems as though Austrians were unduly fastidious in this respect. The same conducteur recalled a millionaire who declined to eat the dishes served on the Orient

Express but went to the enormous expense of having a full seven-course dinner prepared for him personally in the kitchens of the internationally known Hotel Sacher, in Vienna, and brought to the Hauptbahnhof every time he passed through the station on one of his long train journeys. It took all the self-restraint the Orient Express chef possessed to accept this implied snub to the excellence of his kitchen and his own recognised competence.

Some of the great Hungarian and Rumanian landowners travelled almost like Royalty. They had their entourage not merely of wives and offspring but of valets and ladies'-maids and other servants; they lived aboard the Orient Express almost as though they were in their own magnificent castles, surrounded by limitless acres of hunting terrain. It would not have entirely surprised the chefs-de-train if these haughty individuals had demanded that the train be stopped so that they could alight and do some shooting before continuing on their way. Had there existed such things as horse-boxes in those days it is more than probable that they might have done so!

Some of these gentry insisted, like the Maharajah of Rana Bahadour, on having their own chefs with them. They would charter a special dining-car, install their chef, and devise their own menus. They often had their dogs with them, and installed an assistant chef to cater for their needs. One conducteur recalls that the Company for a time attached a special fourgon for these dogs, so numerous had they become. The dogs' favourite dish, it appeared, was Viennese *naturschnitzel*—a dish that many travellers would regard as a luxury if it appeared on their own plates. The Company did not mind: if a passenger was prepared to pay, over and above the normal fare and the supplementary fare, the sum of several thousand francs or dinars in order to satisfy such whims—well, why not let him?

There are less spectacular but more amusing anecdotes to be found among these conducteurs' jottings: the affair of the decree about Turkish headgear, for instance.

For centuries all Turks had worn the traditional fez, or tarboosh. But when Kemal Ataturk became President of the new Republic of Turkey and set about Westernising the country (as well as moving the capital and seat of government east from Constantinople to Ankara), one of the first edicts that he issued was that the fez was to be abolished and all Turks must forthwith wear some form of headgear in the Western tradition. He would brook no protest over this; already he was well on his way to becoming a dictator, and his word was virtually law.

Turkish outfitters were faced at once with a formidable problem. Moreover, it was a problem that had to be solved immediately. So, requests were sent through to Europe for the prompt despatch of as many hats of all kinds as the hatters of the various nations could produce from stock. These were assembled at a central point, in Paris of course, and loaded on to the Orient Express for the swiftest possible delivery.

The chef-de-train recalled the consignment as the strangest one he ever had to accept aboard his luxury train. Into the rear fourgon went hundreds and thousands of samples of Western European headgear. There were tall hats and bowlers, felt hats in all shapes and sizes, homburgs and tam-o'-shanters, forage-caps and Balaclavas, slouch hats and opera hats, straw hats and Panamas, smoking-caps and pork-pie hats, boaters and Basque bérets and billycocks, trilbies and Tyrolean hats, wide-awakes and glengarries; there was hardly a hat known to Europeans that was not included in this enormous consignment for delivery to the unsuspecting Turks.

Kemal Ataturk's so-called Hat Law was keenly resented by the Turks. And no wonder. For when this motley array of headgear came to be distributed the streets must have presented a most extraordinary spectacle: Orient and Occident had met and been most strangely, uncomfortably, blended! The Turkish male felt that he was from then onwards deprived of all dignity. 'Headgear,' said an observer who was present at the time, 'which used to distinguish the true Turk from the Christian, became a class badge. It was a case of cloth cap for the peasant and working-man and brimmed hat for Effendi. Ataturk's Hat Law aroused the greatest possible resentment.'

The conducteurs and chefs-de-train, of course, would not be aware of this: their job was to deliver the goods and to turn the train round in readiness for the journey back to Paris.

One conducteur recalls a curious experience he had during the heyday of the Orient Express, when there seemed to be no end to the remarkable characters whose names appeared on his passenger-lists. Among these one day was the name Basil Zaharoff. Zaharoff had been born of Greek parents in a poor quarter of Constantinople. But he had from the first shown that he had the makings in him of an astute businessman, and almost before he had ceased to be a boy he had entered the field of armaments manufacturing and very soon became, in the words of a jealous and bitter rival, 'Monarch of the Kingdom of Cannon Manufacturers'.

Like many successful businessmen, he was a restless individual, and had a tendency to insomnia. This conducteur recalls how he used to wander up and down the corridors of the train, unable to sleep for the business worries that continuously revolved in his mind. One night, it seems, he was wandering through the wagon-lits adjacent to his own when he heard a wild shriek, and a door burst open right in front of him. Before he knew what was happening, a young woman flung herself into his arms, screaming hysterically: 'Save me! My husband has gone mad! He has just tried to murder me! Save me . . . Save me!'

Zaharoff was a man of action as well as an astute businessman. Sweeping the young woman behind him, he smote the man who was peering out of the compartment a heavy blow on the nose, and then made for his own compartment with the young woman still clinging to him. By then the conducteur had appeared on the scene, and he interposed himself between the outraged husband and the hysterical woman and her rescuer, while they locked themselves into his compartment. Gradually the woman calmed down, and was able to tell her story. Her name, she informed Zaharoff, was Maria de Pilar Angel-Patricimio Simona del Mugniso y Berrete. Only that morning she had been married, against her will, to the man who had just tried to murder her. In telling her sad story it looked as though she was going to break out in another fit of hysterics. Basil Zaharoff did his utmost to comfort her and get her to relax.

What had begun as drama was to end in romance. Zaharoff fell in love with the young woman with the formidably long name. He had immense financial resources, and succeeded in persuading the husband to release her. No sooner was she released than she became Zaharoff's wife. The wife, incidentally, of a man so wealthy that on more than one occasion he put his signature to a cheque for over £1,000,000! He never revealed the size of the cheque that he had to pay for the woman he had rescued; but, the conducteur added wryly, it was clearly money well spent.

It was another conducteur on this same train who tells the story of a puzzling passenger who once came under his care. This individual refused to allow him, or any other member of the train staff, to handle a bundled-up carpet that he was carrying when he came aboard the Orient Express in Constantinople to make the long journey westwards to Paris. In his experience, every passenger on this luxury train always made a point of handing over even the lightest of his pieces of baggage before climbing the steps into the train; but—not this passenger!

Puzzled, the conducteur consulted his passenger-list. The name given on it was Calouste Sarkis Gulbenkian. A conducteur always knows more than might be expected, and though this was the first time he had this passenger aboard his train he knew very well that he was the son-in-law of a landowner who had extensive oil-wells in and around Baku. He guessed, and rightly, that young Calouste Gulbenkian was travelling west on his father-in-law's business: probably to arrange some financial transaction that would be to his benefit first and foremost, and only afterwards to the benefit of those with whom he had dealings. (This, in fact, was the man who in due course was to be popularly known as 'Mr Five-per-cent' because of his genius for extracting a commission on every business deal in which he took part, whether on his own or on someone else's behalf.)

At that time, however, he was by no means a wealthy man. He depended on the occasional help of his wife's wealthy father, for he had no very remunerative job of his own. If he could succeed in what he was setting out to do, then things might look up very nicely in the future. Meanwhile, all he could do was to live in hope. He had been given a ticket on the Orient Express to go to Paris and if possible do a deal there on his father-in-law's behalf. He was to try to make contact with the immensely wealthy family of Rothschilds, and persuade them to put money into the oil business by offering his father-in-law a substantial sum for the first claim on the products of his oil-bearing land in the district of Baku.

The conducteur solved the mystery of the rolled-up carpet when he happened to look in on his passenger and found him—unwrapping a very small boy from its folds!

'M'sieur, why . . . ?' The conducteur was astonished by what he saw.

Calouste Sarkis Gulbenkian 'came clean'. It was necessary to get his small son to Paris, for a reason which he would rather not explain. He had only been given enough money for his own fare, so, since he could not afford a ticket for his son, he had had to secrete him in the folds of this carpet. The ruse had unfortunately been exposed as a result of the conducteur's unexpected visit to the compartment. So . . . ?

He had an engaging manner, a persuasive smile. And it happened that the conducteur had a son of his own, of just about the little chap's age. He would, he said, exercise his right of discretion, and say nothing about this to the chef-de-train—his superior—though Company's regulations were that any problem should be handed over to him. Meanwhile, he would see what he could do about finding something for the little chap to eat. And the father was not to worry himself: all would be arranged.

The kindly conducteur was as good as his word. He obtained food from the kitchen that was suitable for a small child, and in a dozen different ways made things easier for the young and harassed father. And, what was more, he actually put some business in the young man's way. 'That beautiful Armenian carpet, m'sieur,' he said, tentatively. 'I think I could find you a buyer for that who would be willing to pay a handsome price. Indeed, I know just the man, and he is on board the train at this very moment. We will wait until we arrive at the Gare de l'Est, and then the transaction shall be made!'

It proved to be the turn of the tide for young Calouste Sarkis Gulbenkian. He sold his carpet at a price so high that even he, with the love of bargaining that is inborn in every Oriental, whether from Japan and China or Armenia and Turkey, had no wish to haggle. And he had the good sense to give the friendly conducteur a handsome commission for the trouble he had taken in the matter, and the discretion he had exercised. This was already part of his business creed: a policy that was to make him one of the richest men the world has ever known.

As for the objective of his railway journey: he made contact with the businessmen he had been sent to negotiate with, first in Paris and then in London. From his negotiations there eventually resulted the vast Royal Dutch Shell Oil merger, in which many hundreds of thousands of pounds and guilders changed hands. From this vast transaction the astute Gulbenkian demanded his five-per-cent commission, which amounted to a sum that would have enabled him, had he so wished, to have travelled across Europe in a specially chartered Orient Express coach as many times as he liked for the rest of his life. Certainly never again would it have been necessary for him to disguise his son as a rolled-up carpet in order to avoid paying his fare from Constantinople to Paris!

There is really no end to the stories that these chefs-de-train and conducteurs have to tell, for there was no end to the variety of passengers who came under their care. There were, of course, the good and the bad, the distinguished and famous and also the plain notorious; there were men bent on business (and women, too) whose sole use for the Orient Express was to find pleasure and excitement of one sort of another. And there were 'big' businessmen who seemed to prefer doing their business aboard a moving train instead of in an office in the city.

One conducteur had particularly good reason to remember an internationally known Italian financier, for he appeared to run the whole of his vast organisation aboard the Orient Express, though he had headquarters in Milan and other important offices in Turin and Rome, Paris, Brussels and elsewhere throughout Europe.

His regular practice was to engage a complete coach and fill it with his secretaries, his bankers' representatives and other individuals whose knowledge and skills he could make use of. At every station he had a sheaf of telegrams and cables to be sent off, not only all over Europe but across the Atlantic and the Pacific as well. He was 'playing the market' in a big way: dealing in hundreds of thousands of pounds' worth of stocks and shares of every conceivable kind. And when he made 'a big kill', as he humorously used to put it, he would give his conducteur an enormous tip, always in gold coin, to celebrate the occasion. No wonder he was well remembered by this particular conducteur, and that there was keen rivalry among the Company's staff to be appointed to the train when he had his special coach attached to it!

Another very popular passenger—though for a very different reason—was the famous cabaret star, Josephine Baker, whose 'act' consisted of dancing exotic dances while wearing little more than a girdle of ripe bananas strung about her. Not unnaturally she was a hit in every capital in Europe. She is remembered by chefs-de-train and conducteurs on the Orient Express not so much for her fame as for her sheer friendliness as she travelled about Europe, appearing first on one stage and then on another: great success had not spoiled her, as it has spoiled so many stars of stage and screen.

One conducteur had a personal contact with her that he will certainly never forget. One night, between two and three o'clock, somewhere in central Europe, he was wakened from his cat-nap by the bell ringing in his cubby-hole at the end of the corridor of his wagon-lits. He never got more than brief spells of sleep, for passengers tended to stay up late in the wagon-salon, drinking and playing cards and being generally convivial; and even when at long last they had turned in for the night, as likely as not they would ring for something or other. But at this hour in the early morning it was unusual to be disturbed.

The conducteur straightened his tie, and with rather an ill grace, for he had had a hard day and had another ahead of him, pulled on his slippers and made his way along the corridor. The bell had been rung from Compartment 27. It was Josephine Baker's. He tapped lightly on the door, and opened it. '*Madame désire . . .* ?' he began.

'Some sandwiches. Ham. And some orange-juice. I am thirsty, and also hungry.'

'But—madame!' Momentarily the conducteur was annoyed, and justifiably so. He even allowed his annoyance to show momentarily on his face. It was, he felt, unreasonable of any passenger to rouse him with such a request, at such an hour.

'I know. It is late.' Josephine Baker's husky Louisiana voice was warm and ingratiating, her big brown eyes persuasive. 'M. le Conducteur, I promise you I will reward you. Please: those sandwiches, and the orange-juice!'

Conducteurs were accustomed to big tips. They were accustomed, too, to unreasonable requests. This certainly was unreasonable. On the other hand, 'La Bakhair', as she was known to most of them, was a generous tipper. He made a swift mental calculation as he closed the door quietly behind him, and went to the kitchen to cut her ham sandwiches with his own hands. The chef, of course, was fast asleep and must not be disturbed for several hours yet.

Ten minutes later he came quietly back down the corridor, with a plate of neatly cut sandwiches and a glass of orange-juice on a tray, with a folded napkin beside them. He knocked discreetly, and waited.

'*Entrez!*'

He entered. And what confronted him came as so great a surprise that only his inborn gift of discipline prevented him from dropping the tray on the floor. Josephine Baker had donned her internationally famous banana-costume. With a lively twinkle in her eye she proceeded to go through her spectacular act for his benefit and his alone: it was probably the only time she had ever danced to an audience of one; and it was certainly the only time a wagon-lits conducteur had ever been granted such a privilege. He 'dined out' on the story for months afterwards.

Josephine Baker, incidentally, was on board the Orient Express on one of the very few occasions in its long history of transcontinental running when it met with real trouble. Again the train was in central Europe, this time on the Austrian network. It was early evening, and the great cabaret star had been persuaded, not to do her act but to sing some of the songs which she had made so very much her own. A particular favourite among these began: 'I have two Loves—my Country and Paree!'

She had just come to the end of the first line when there was a tremendous explosion somewhere up in the front portion of the train. Brakes were jammed hard on, and everybody in the wagon-salon was precipitated from armchair to carpeted floor as the Orient Express ground to a sudden standstill. Immediately, the chef-de-train appeared in their midst, imploring everyone to remain calm and assuring them that they had nothing at all to worry about.

Josephine Baker, good trouper that she was, launched a second time into her song. Such was her personal magnetism that very soon she had her audience one and all beneath her spell, completely silent till she came to the end of the last verse, when applause broke out that drowned the commotion at the far end of the train.

It transpired that a bomb had exploded as the engine passed over it, wrecking the tender and the front fourgon.

The engine itself, which, miraculously, had not been damaged, had to be uncoupled and continue on its way alone, to fetch assistance so that the train journey could be resumed. What was behind all this? There were no wars in progress just then, and the country in which the outrage had been perpetrated was Austria, not one of the smaller, more inflammable Balkan states.

The truth did not come to light for several months, when the Austrian police eventually ran the culprit to earth. He proved to be an Austrian ex-officer named Matusca, recently dismissed from his regiment on a charge of being mentally unbalanced and therefore no longer fit for responsibility. He made no attempt to deny his guilt. In fact, he seemed to take a curious pleasure in admitting to what he had done. Asked what his motive was, he gave an unexpected and quite extraordinary reply: 'I just happen,' he said, quietly, 'not to like the Orient Express.'

Among the international entertainers on a more high-brow level than that of 'La Bakhair' who travelled a great deal in Europe was the great violinist, Jacques Thibaud. He was born only a year or two before the Orient Express itself was born, and died tragically in an airplane crash. 'He would have done better,' said a conducteur who had often looked after him, 'to have remained faithful to the train.' This same conducteur recalled how the great violinist used to refer to himself as 'a grass-hopper that spends his whole life touring on the four strings of his violin'.

On one of these long journeys Thibaud was drowsing when the Orient Express pulled in to Vienna's Haupt-bahnhof. He woke with a start, the alarm-clock in his brain reminding him that he was due to give a recital in the city. Still not fully awake, he stumbled down on to the platform and hurried away from the train, leaving his belongings behind him in his compartment. Fortunately the conducteur, who had been momentarily occupied with another passenger, caught sight of the violinist hurrying, baggage-less, across the station, and was characteristically alert-minded enough to take in the situation.

There was no time to be lost, for the train halted only a matter of minutes in the station and already Thibaud was receding into the distance, dodging through the crowds. The conducteur darted into his compartment and snatched up the large, ungainly piece of luggage which, he knew, contained the violinist's instruments. It was a specially designed case, constructed so as to contain two violins placed head to tail. Calling to a porter to take charge of the rest of the baggage, he raced after Thibaud, to catch up with him just as he was hailing a cab to drive him to his hotel.

'M'sieur!' he called out. 'You have forgotten . . .'

He got no farther. It was though something had suddenly clicked in the violinist's brain and he had returned, as it were, 'to earth'. '*Mon Dieu!*' exclaimed Jacques Thibaud, practically falling backwards off the step of the cab. 'My violins! Quick! Stop the train!'

The conducteur calmed him down sufficiently to look at what he was carrying: the precious dual violin case. 'I have them here, m'sieur,' he said, gently, soothingly. 'Your precious Stradivarius and your no less precious Amati—your beloved violin family!'

Thibaud's two violins were worth who knows how many million francs, for they were the masterpieces of two of

Italy's greatest violin-makers; only a virtuoso like himself could possibly afford to own such treasures. He fumbled in his pocket. 'My friend, I have not sufficient money to repay you for such a service as you have just performed,' he stammered.

'It is my pleasure, m'sieur,' replied the conducteur, and began to walk away, for he had other duties to perform and his train would soon be leaving the Hauptbahnhof. The porter had loaded the rest of the baggage on to the cab, and the driver was looking down inquiringly.

But as he turned away, he heard Thibaud speaking again, and this time in a mock-angry tone: 'You evidently do not know what these are worth to me, M'sieur le Conducteur. Give me your address at once, so that I can send you what I choose to send. If you do not, I shall report you to La Compagnie for disobeying one of its customers!'

Wisely (and probably not unwillingly!) the conducteur gave in. He scribbled down his address on a slip of paper, and handed it politely to Jacques Thibaud. A week later an envelope was awaiting him on his return from a trans-European journey. It contained five 1,000-franc notes. Clipped to them was a card bearing the words '*Merci—cinq mille fois!*' and signed 'Jacques Thibaud'. When he tells the story the wagon-lits conducteur always adds a little postscript: 'Me,' he says, 'I do not understand music. But it seems that music is a *noise which pays*!'

10

Winter, 1929

Considering the enormous mileage covered by the Orient Express on its regular transcontinental journeys, and the sort of terrain over which its tracks lay between Paris and Constantinople, it is surprising that it was so rarely involved in any sort of accident. During the early years of this century, when it had been established for two or three decades, it was running no fewer than four times weekly over the whole route, in each direction; and a subsidiary of the train was being routed three times weekly to Constantza, a port on the Black Sea coast of Rumania a hundred and fifty miles east of Bucharest.

But there was a derailment at Vitry-le-François, a hundred miles east of Paris, which made the headlines of the day, as much as anything because it was the crack Orient Express that was involved, and not simply an ordinary train covering a less important route.

It was twenty minutes to three o'clock on a bleak November morning. A local freight train was stationary on the line, some distance from the station. For some reason that was never satisfactorily explained the driver had brought it to a halt, not on the siding where it should have been until the westbound Orient Express had roared by on the last hundred miles or so of its mammoth journey to the fringe of Asia and back again, but on the main line. There, with black smoke rising lazily from the engine's smoke-stack, the freight train squatted on the rails, weighed down with some hundreds of tons of concrete piles, bags of cement and a consignment of pig-iron. The engine driver was snatching an illegal forty winks, having ordered his young fireman to keep an eye open for the moment when the line should be clear for him to proceed. That moment was not to come.

The Orient Express was travelling fast over a level length of line, making up for a delay of half an hour that had been none of its driver's fault but the result of some confusion over signals nearly a hundred miles further to the east. Drivers of this crack transcontinental train took great pride in maintaining their schedule as laid down by La Compagnie Internationale: if moments were lost *en route*, then they must somehow be made up in order that the train should come to a halt, at either end of the long line, at the scheduled hour.

There was no moon; there were no stars; but there was a thin mist, through which the driver and his fireman, when he was not stoking the furnace, peered keenly ahead. Not that they had anything to fear: this line was a clear one, open to the Orient Express, westbound, and to no other train at that hour. The driver glanced at his big watch, and nodded with pleasure when he saw that he had already made up some of the lost time. He had little doubt that he would make up the remainder of it in the next hundred miles ahead of him. If only the mist would clear, he muttered beneath his breath. Though he knew the line well, and knew from the time-table that it would be clear for him, nevertheless he was easier in his mind when he could see it stretching away into the distance. November, as he knew well, was a bad month for mist and fog.

And then—it happened! Where, seconds before, he had seen that the line immediately ahead of him was clear, as he had been notified by the green signal at Vitry-le-François station that it would be, now there was a wholly unexpected obstruction immediately ahead of him.

Instinctively he throttled down and shut off steam, applying the engine's brakes with all the force at his command. But it was too late. The fifty yards or so that lay between him and the obstruction, whatever it might be, that he had just spotted, were all too little for the Orient Express to be brought to a halt. He yelled to his fireman to jump for his life, and himself stuck to his controls as a ship's captain stands by his ship. The fireman jumped clear and rolled down the embankment to the left of the train. The driver, as his engine ran slap into the rear of the immobilised freight train, was thrown hard up against the front of his cab and fatally injured. The engine piled into the rear wagons of the freight train, half climbing over them as it crushed them beneath its wheels. The fourgon immediately behind the tender—the all-important fourgon that carried the international mails—was driven forward by the weight of the heavy sleeping-cars and dining-car behind it and piled up over the tender and the cab of the engine with the dead driver. The sheer weight of the piled-up engine, fourgon and freight wagons proved too much for the line itself, which at this point ran along an embankment. It sagged and gave way. The wrecked engine, the freight wagons into which it had so violently ploughed, and the mail fourgon and tender with which they had become inextricably involved, tipped off the line and rolled down the embankment in one enormous cluster of mangled metal and timber. The night was made hideous by the bursting of a steam-pipe and the banshee scream of escaping high-pressure steam. The fireman, who had jumped from the cab at his driver's orders, and rolled forwards as well as downwards over the embankment, was caught by the falling mass of engine and wagons, and crushed to death in seconds.

Fortunately the couplings behind the mail fourgon had parted, or the sleeping-cars and diner, too, would have followed engine and tender and mail fourgon down the embankment and the consequent loss of life might have been formidable. As it was, they stayed upright on the line, though quivering throughout their length with the force of the impact that had brought them to a halt, and the unevenness of the track beneath them. Shaken and shocked, passengers could see in the half-light through their windows the tumbled heap of rolling-stock that had somersaulted down the embankment and come to rest in the ravine at its foot. It was an ugly sight, and one from which they were glad enough to turn away.

The noise of the collision had of course brought the station staff and others hurrying and stumbling along the line in the misty darkness, dreading what they might find on arrival. Each man carried a storm-lantern, and it was an eerie sight as they stumbled along, their lanterns swinging like a line of half-crazed giant glow-worms. The banshee wail of the escaping steam was now dying down as the pressure dropped in the steam-pipe, and the air was now filled with shouts and cries from the frightened

12. *Wagon-Restaurant* in 1906

13. The Orient Express in 1912

14. Derailment of the Orient Express at Vitry le François in 1911

passengers, who had no means of being sure that the line might not give way and precipitate them down the embankment to join the smashed and mangled wagons piled on top of one another in the ravine. The task of quieting them fell to the conducteurs and chef-de-train, who performed it with their customary tact and skill. Their baggage was collected, and they were led back along the line to the station at Vitry-le-François, where they were given hot drinks and soothed and assured that every care would be taken of them and that they would be put on the road for their destination with the least possible delay. It had been a terrifying experience, and one that neither train staff nor passengers ever wanted to repeat.

As was customary, the chef-de-train made his official report to his Company. The fourgon, that all-important mail-carrying fourgon, he had to state, was shattered beyond repair. In accordance with the regulations laid down by the Company for just such an emergency—though it was one that all hoped would never occur—the shattered fourgon's parts would be carefully collected and despatched for inspection in a special wagon that would be obtained for the purpose. Thus the court of inquiry would have everything to hand for their purposes. The wagon would be sealed with the Company's seal, and put under the guardianship of a reliable member of the staff.

The report went on to the effect that the wagon-restaurant was badly damaged, one of its two bogies having been smashed and an axle having risen through the floor of the coach and splintered it throughout almost its entire length. On the brighter side he was able to report that, shock and fright and a bruise or two apart, not one of the passengers had been a casualty. On the darker side, a Serbian conducteur who happened to be on duty in the fore part of the train had been killed, as also had the driver and fireman of the locomotive. It was a mystery as to why this particular servant of the Company had been killed, but it appeared that he had been passing between one coach and the next and must have been hit by a stone dislodged from the track, or by something—perhaps a lump of coal—shooting out of the tender ahead.

Perhaps even more mysterious was the fact that a member of the train's staff essentially responsible for the safety of the mail carried in the mail fourgon, who had actually been in the fourgon when it was catapulted down the embankment and shattered in the bottom of the ravine—actually survived! And survived in sufficiently good trim to write out an on-the-spot report of what had happened to the mail fourgon for which he was responsible. It is a remarkable illustration of *sang-froid* in what must have been quite terrifying circumstances, and deserves to be quoted as he set it down that same night as he sipped a cup of cocoa in the station-master's office at Vitry-le-François . . .

I was on duty [Postier Maumy wrote in his official report] when the mail-fourgon overturned down the embankment as a result of the violent collision. Finding myself trapped in my cabin, I forced a way out for myself through the débris. Having extricated myself, I then remained alongside the overturned and shattered fourgon, as I was at that time responsible for the safety of the postal bags. I awaited anxiously the arrival of some employees of the Serbian Postal Department, who must share the responsibility. There were 132 bags in all, of which 8 were destined for Ljubljana. To my regret, I was quite unable to find in my cabin a number of postal documents connected with the delivery of bags handed in to my care at Plovdiv, Sofia, Tzarisbrod and Belgrade, my cabin having been reduced to matchwood by the violence of the accident. Happily no damage seems to have been sustained by the bags themselves. Nor, I am happy to report, was I myself injured—apart from minor bruises and scratches. . . .

Certainly it was something of a miracle, for the mail fourgon was in fact, as he described it, reduced to matchwood. He must have borne a charmed life!

This official report by the man-on-the-spot emphasises once again the essential loyalty of the staff of La Compagnie Générale des Wagons-Lits et des Grands Express Européens. It is a reminder, too, of the importance that has always been attached to the carrying of mail since the inaugural run so many years before, when the fourgon immediately behind the little 'Est' 2—4—0 carried international mail for the first time from one side of Europe to the other.

But of all the hazards with which the Orient Express had to contend, the worst, without question, was bad weather. In two-thousand-odd miles the train ran over plains and plateaux, along valleys and over high passes, exchanging as it did so the comparatively mild weather of Paris for the ice and frost and snow of central Europe and the blizzards sweeping westwards out of Russia, across the Black Sea, into Turkey-in-Europe. It was always a prolonged journey. When the route was inaugurated in 1883 it took over eighty hours; ten years later the time had been reduced to sixty-five hours—just over two days and a half;

ten years later still, with heavier and more powerful locomotives, another five hours had been lopped off the time between western and eastern termini. But there were still three nights and two intervening days to be passed in the train.

Elderly and retired railwaymen still talk of the year 1929 as one of the grimmest in their experience; particularly the month of February. It was the winter when axle-boxes froze solid; when even the bottles of wine carried on the train froze, and the wine-waiters had to 'open' them by breaking off their necks and then thawing out the contents in the kitchen! The archives of the Company contain numberless records of the conditions in which their long-distance trains were obliged to run.

Reports were sent through the various European headquarters from key-points all over the Continent. The authorities were thus enabled to keep tabs on the conditions that the drivers and firemen and others would be forced to contend with. One of these reports gives a very clear picture indeed of the conditions prevailing on 13th February of that terrible year. The writer of the report stated that as a result of the continued fall in temperature ('−35° has been recorded in Transilvania and −28° at Bucharest') the movement of trains was becoming increasingly difficult. Owing to the heavy snow and the shortage of engines, shunting and making-up of trains had proved almost impossible. Several times, he went on, it had been necessary to manhandle coaches in and out of their sheds, using squads of twenty or thirty cleaners at a time, when they could be obtained. Trains on branch-lines had had to be cancelled altogether, in many cases, as it had proved impossible to shift snow on the tracks. Another trouble was that engines froze up owing to the extreme shortage of fuel. A considerable number of wagons had either frozen up solid or had their heating-systems irreparably damaged in their desperate attempts to get them to function. Wash-basins and W.C.s froze up and split, for it had proved impossible to maintain a flow of warm, let alone hot, water through them. It was so cold that even warm water froze as soon as it emerged from the taps. In brief, it was an impossible situation with which they were confronted.

It was not only the rolling-stock that was affected by these appalling weather conditions: railwaymen in all grades, came the report to the Company, were being badly affected by them. Train staff and others were exhausted by the demands made on them to maintain even a skeleton service. They were having to forgo their statutory rest periods because train schedules had gone hopelessly awry and trains were taking far longer over each section of the route than had been allowed for in the time-tables.

Worse, there were accidents immediately resulting from these weather conditions. A member of the railway staff broke an ankle when he slipped on an ice-coated step. Another, a conducteur this time, had a frost-bitten ear as a result of looking out of a window while his train was in motion. Even the toughest central European staff, more accustomed than those from farther west to snow and ice and blizzards, were succumbing to the effects of their ordeal. On one service alone, two conducteurs, named as Drossu and Priboianu, were on the sick-list. Another, named Glovaci, had to be taken to hospital in Vienna, transported in his own bunk removed from staff sleeping-quarters and accompanied by a fellow-member of the staff to make sure that nothing worse happened to him *en route*.

Passengers were quick to complain—as though the Company's devoted servants were responsible for the weather and the inconvenience it caused. Why, they demanded angrily of the conducteurs and chefs-de-train, was there not plenty of hot water circulating in the heating-system and flowing through the taps in the sleeping-coaches?

Some passengers, to the Company's great distress, did not confine their complaints to the ears of the train staff: worse, they wrote letters of complaint to the editors of various newspapers. One editor collected as many of these unreasonable complaints as came to his desk in one week, and had an article written-up for his paper, based on them. It duly appeared under a banner headline designed to catch everyone's eye:

HOW ONE TRAVELS IN TODAY'S COLD WEATHER

The article began with the uncompromising statement: 'A journey in the wagon-lits today is a misery!' It ended with a challenge: 'This state of confusion should be brought to an end, NOW!' The body of the article contained matter that caused the greatest possible distress to the Company, which was at once justifiably proud of the service it had been offering to long-distance passengers for almost half a century, and helpless in the face of such extreme weather conditions. It read with great concern the blunt protests of its passengers, who had written: 'Surely the hazards of frozen points could have been foreseen and prevented?' And: 'There should be plenty of coaches held in reserve, so that when the heating breaks down in one, another can be substituted. Passengers who pay for expensive tickets ought to be GUARANTEED comfort and immunity from disorganisation.' But there was little that could be done about this in a winter such as that of 1929.

Perhaps over the years passengers had become spoiled. Certainly this particular passenger had no idea of the care and devotion to duty that was characteristic of the employees of La Compagnie, of the frantic efforts they were all making to overcome the almost insuperable obstacles presented by the weather conditions of that bitter and never-to-be-forgotten February. It was as well for him that he was not travelling on the Orient Express that set out from the Gare de l'Est, Paris, one evening in the last week of January of that year. Had he been doing so, he really would have had something to complain about.

There were eighty passengers on the Orient Express when it set out from Paris, but only a quarter of these had booked right through to Constantinople. The remainder were leaving the train at various stations along the route: at Munich and Vienna, Budapest and Belgrade and Sofia, and at some of the smaller stations in between these. They little knew how fortunate they were that their journeys were to end before they crossed the last frontier, out of Bulgaria into Turkey.

The passenger-list was the customary 'mixed bag'. There were a number of businessmen. There were several diplomats, including members of the British and French Legations in Turkey. There was a French engineer returning to Turkey after consulting his firm about a proposed waterworks project which he had been commissioned to execute.

There was a Turk named Souf who from the very outset gave the impression of wishing to keep himself to himself. He declined to enter into conversation with his fellow-passengers, either at meal-times or between meals, prefering to bury himself deep in newspapers. He wore the *babouche*, the traditional Turkish soft slipper, and tended, as some of the others casually noted, to sit with his feet hidden beneath the rug he always had with him. It was suggested by one of the passengers that he might be a smuggler. The suggestion was made as a joke; but in fact, on a later trip, back from the East to Paris, he was arrested by Customs and Excise officers and found to be carrying several hundred grains of cocaine secreted between the thin soles of each *babouche*.

There were very few women passengers. One of these was an Austrian, an attractive young woman named von Werner, travelling unaccompanied. This laid a heavy burden of responsibility on the chef-de-train when the crisis arose, for these excellent servants of La Compagnie always made it their business to look after any passenger who had no escort and seemed therefore to be in particular need of surveillance. There were a couple of Jesuit priests who, like M. Souf, though for very different reasons, kept themselves to themselves. They spent their whole time reading out of massive black-printed Bibles, not laying them on one side even at meal-times. The passengers who occupied the compartment next to theirs in the wagon-lits complained to their conducteur that they were kept awake the whole night through by the two men incessantly reading aloud to one another. It was a great relief to the other passengers when the two priests alighted somewhere in Hungary and were seen no more. Three wealthy and widely travelled Parisian couples, whose goal was a hydropathic establishment built in the mountains and run as a profitable side-line by the Company, seemed to be the only passengers among the original eighty who were not bound on some sort of business. But they, too, left part way along the route; only twenty-odd of the eighty ticket-holders were booked right through.

A few snowflakes had been falling when the Orient Express emerged from the tunnel outside the Gare de l'Est, heading eastwards. By the time the German frontier was reached, it was real snow. In Austria the train was running over a landscape white from horizon to horizon, a snowy sheet made the more dazzling by contrast with the endless forests of larch and pine. The track itself was a twin black pencil-line between snow that was often banked as high as the sills of the wagon-salon-restaurant windows.

It was quite enjoyable, some of the passengers remarked amiably to one another, to sit behind those windows, warmed by the very efficient steam-heating of this luxury express, and look out over the snow-clad landscape over which they were being transported in such comfort. And fast, too. For the gallant little 'Est' 2—4—0 which had hauled the Orient Express on its inaugural run had long since been replaced by a much more powerful 'Est' 4—4—0; and even this more powerful locomotive had been replaced by the newly designed 4—6—0 Series II, a giant by the standards of those far-off days. That remarkable locomotive came to be known by the railwaymen over the whole vast network in Europe as 'le Ten-Wheel'.

There was thick ice on the Danube where it flowed sluggishly between the twin cities of Buda and Pest. When they were midway across the huge Hungarian plain to the south-east, serpentining rivers like the Tisza and the Koros lay like tangled rivers of grey silk in the limitless expanse of virgin snow. Venturesome passengers who left the snug warmth of their parlour-car for a momentary breath of fresh air found that a few seconds of such Spartan indulgence were more than enough. Not many were so foolhardy as to do this. One of them was a young British courier travelling out to his embassy with the diplomatic bags. But even he gave up the suicidal practice when the train came within range of the mountains. And no one was more pleased when he gave up this foolish practice of his than the humble member of the train staff whose duty it was to keep up the supply of steam for the heating-system in the coaches; for when the ice-cold air was permitted to invade the corridors through an open window his task was made almost impossible.

When it had crossed the Rumanian frontier the Orient Express was caught in what seemed to be a two-pronged attack of wintry wind: a wind from the east, blowing right in its teeth, and a wind from the north which had picked up the unbelievable cold of Russia. A temperature as low as 40 degrees of frost had been reported only that week from Chernovtsy, on the frontier of Rumania and the Ukraine. These fearful winds came scudding down upon the track like a gigantic scythe-edge to mow down the Orient Express as it fought its way eastwards to the Bosporus. There was only one grain of comfort that the train staff could offer their passengers: wind as cold as this was unlikely to result in an increase of snow. Chef-de-train and conducteurs alike made this statement with every sign of confidence. Inexperienced travellers drew comfort from the information; the veterans withheld their judgment.

By the time the train had crossed the frontier into Bulgaria its complement of passengers had been reduced to a quarter. Two or three of the wagons-lits had been detached, and the Orient Express was reduced to a ghost of its usual self. There were very few advance bookings for the return journey, at least over the eastern portion of it; extra coaches could be coupled up as the train proceeded farther west through Europe, if the need arose. But now the train was travelling south by east to cross the last frontier: that between Bulgaria and Turkey, between the Stara Planina and the Rhodope Mountains. As it entered Turkey it entered on the final lap of its two-thousand-mile journey; and it was very soon after entering Turkey that disaster befell the Orient Express.

Snow, borne on a strong east wind, had been driving into the wide valley between the two mountain ranges for several weeks. It was not so much falling, as sweeping in from the east: snowflakes as large as goose feathers were massed together so that it seemed as though a million feather pillows were being violently shaken out of the sky, to be whirled in an almost solid mass westwards up the valley. The snow had spread across the landscape, levelling out the rough places, filling in the hollows, so that now a vast undulating blanket reached from horizon to horizon.

This, said the European passengers, peering anxiously through their steamed-up windows, is not snow as we know it. They spoke half fearfully, half admiringly. The handful of Parisian Frenchmen knew snow as something that, for a month or two every winter, descended upon their city, lay thick in their wide boulevards, adorned the shoulders and shields of the statues on the bridges that spanned the Seine and brought a touch of cold beauty to the towers and flying-buttresses of the Cathedral of Notre Dame. But this snow: this was something none of them had ever seen before.

There were, of course, no landmarks by which the speed of their train could any longer be judged. However, it did not require an expert's ear to detect that the speed of the train had diminished to little more than a crawl. The double thud-thud of the bogies hitting the joints between the rails had slowed down to such an extent that some passengers held their breath waiting for the next to occur. The thought came into the mind of first one passenger and then another that the train might possibly be brought to a standstill by the sheer weight of snow against which it had now been battling for so long. They glanced furtively at one another to see whether their fears were shared; and they derived no comfort from the exchange of such glances.

Nor did they derive any more comfort from the members of the train staff whom they encountered in the wagon-salon or the corridors. It was evident that they were making a brave effort to look unconcerned; but it did not require much imagination to detect that the conducteurs, the chef-de-train himself, were very worried indeed.

The intervals between the thud-thud of the bogies became longer and longer; and then—an interval became so long that in fact it did not end at all: the Orient Express had at last ground to a halt. Above the hiss of driven snow sweeping viciously against the steamy windows of the coach could now be heard the blast of escaping steam from the 'Est' 4—6—0, the famous 'Ten-Wheel', at the head of the diminished train. For a moment or two the silent passengers listened to it as though it was something they had never heard before. And then the blast of steam itself was reduced to a hiss that was soon absorbed into that of the driving snow; an uncanny and rather frightening silence filled the train.

From the Turco-Bulgarian frontier to the Bosporus was rather more than a hundred and fifty miles. Stations were few and far between. Passengers who had travelled that stretch of track before recalled that the country through which it passed was singularly empty. It was a region of small farms scattered thinly over a vast area of waste land. Even in fair weather it could hardly be called prepossessing; in conditions such as those in which they now found themselves it was dismal indeed. For all they could tell from the non-existent landmarks they might as well be on the last lap to the North or the South Pole! They shivered at the thought, and looked at one another and at their conducteurs for comfort; and comfort was not forthcoming.

Where, they speculated, were they in that waste land? They could not even see it clearly, for the snow was driving across it like an army of white-clad ghost-horsemen. The last station they had passed through, someone said, was Tcherkeuy (also called Tcherkesskeuy). But it was little more than a wayside halt, for the village contained only a few hundred inhabitants at most. And anyway: how long ago was it that their train had passed through that halt? In conditions such as these, time-tables had been abandoned, and time and distance themselves were two elements that were quite impossible to assess. And for that matter, was it, now, of any real importance to them?

The English diplomatic courier, with those important diplomatic bags in his charge, was inclined to think that it was. He said he would go and seek out the chef-de-train and tell him that in his opinion the best thing now was to put the train in reverse and back it along the line westwards to Tcherkeuy. After all, they knew there was such a place behind them, whereas none of them knew what lay ahead of them—even supposing the train could be set in motion once more. At least, he pointed out, by going into reverse they would be helped rather than hindered by the blizzard from the east. Convinced that he had found the answer to the problem, the young courier set off along the corridor to put his case to the chef-de-train and his colleagues.

He found the entire train crew in conference. The driver and fireman had left the footplate of 'le Ten-Wheel' and managed somehow to make their way back over the tender, scrambling over the heaped briquettes of coal, down on to the coupling, past the leading mail-fourgon and so to the chef-de-train's quarters in the next coach. To enter it they had had to tear away the accumulated hard-packed snow and lever open the coach door, which was frozen tight shut. A whirl of icy snow followed them into the coach, and the two men were glad to thaw out their numbed fingertips on the chef-de-train's stove. The snow, they reported ominously, was now level with the tops of the bogies and beginning to wedge beneath the floor of the coaches.

The diplomatic courier came out with his suggestion

that the train should at once be put into reverse and backed along the track to Tcherkeuy. The chef-de-train, courteous as all the Company's employees were trained to be, thanked him for his suggestion and said it would receive immediate consideration. The courier, having put forward his proposal, and recognising that he was a layman among professionals, tactfully withdrew to report to his fellow-passengers that his suggestion had been well received.

But when the chef-de-train came through, half an hour later, to the parlour-car his face was grave. The situation, he told them as they fell silent at his approach, was indeed serious. There was no question of moving either forwards or backwards, for the train was completely snow-locked. Snow covered the line and was fast building up on either side of the coaches. It was falling with unprecedented weight and speed. In many years of travelling over this route he himself had never seen its like. If messieurs les voyageurs would condescend to look out of the windows they would see for themselves that the snow was piling up almost visibly; it was now approaching the sill of the coach windows. Further movement was quite impossible. He regretted the circumstances infinitely, but—alas—Nature now had the upper hand.

'Then,' said the diplomatic courier briskly, with a quick glance round for approval, 'we must summon assistance, and with the least possible delay. The situation in which we find ourselves is not to be tolerated a moment longer than is necessary.'

The chef-de-train regarded him in silence for a moment or two. Then, speaking gently but firmly, he said: 'Alas, m'sieur, I fear this is impossible. There is no means of sending a message. The telegraph-lines are down all along the track, thanks to the weight of the snow and the force of the blizzard. We cannot get a message either forward to our destination or even the few miles back along the line to Tcherkeuy. In a word, messieurs,' he ended, facing the passengers as a whole, 'we are marooned.'

15. *Wagon-Restaurant*, in which the Armistice was signed, at Les Invalides in 1921

16. The Orient Express snowed-up at Tcherkesskeuy (Tcherkeuy) in February 1929

Nous voyageurs du "Simplon-Express" No. 3 le considérons comme notre devoir de certifier que le personnel du train resté bloqué dans la neige à Tcherkesskeuy durant cinq jours et par un temps épouvantable a fait des efforts surhumains afin que la commodité des voyageurs ait à souffrir le moins possible. Au risque de leur santé ils sont montés sur les toits des wagons en pleine tempête afin de les approvisionner d'eau, et, manquant de charbon, tous, sans exception, ont fait leur devoir jusqu'au bout.

Tcherkesskeuy, 5 Février 1929

17. The certificate of gratitude to the Orient Express staff, signed by the passengers on the train snowed up at Tcherkesskeuy (Tcherkeuy)

11

Deep-freeze in Turkey

The passengers assembled in the parlour-car looked at one another, horrified. Marooned: this was worse than the worst of their fears. They were a lost community, isolated from the rest of their world, unable to make contact with their fellow-men; their very lives, then, were at hazard! The chef-de-train soothingly assured them that he and his most competent staff would do everything in their power to make conditions as endurable, indeed as comfortable, for them as they possibly could. Meanwhile, of course, they must not worry. All would be well, they might rest assured.

The ugly word 'marooned' faded from their consciousness. The tradition of service and efficiency aboard these long-distance trains was now well established; of course they need not worry! The experienced passengers on board reminded the others that there were always ample provisions of all sorts in the rear stores-fourgon, for menus were always variegated as well as lavish. The young Englishman was overheard to remark that a touch of the unexpected, even a threat of discomfort or danger, added spice to what might otherwise be mere routine. No one else among the passengers, however, seemed to agree with him on this last point. And for a day and a night, anyway, no one felt—or at least no one registered—any real hint of anxiety. No one, that is, except Fräulein von Werner, whose attractive dark brown eyes had clouded with apprehension at the news given them by the chef-de-train. She was rather an emotional young woman, and more than one of her fellow-passengers suspected that they might have trouble with her if things became really difficult.

On the third day, to everyone's relief, the snow ceased to fall. But by now the level was higher than the roof of the train. It had long been impossible to see out of the windows. The only way the depth of the snow could be ascertained was by probing with a long pole, a chilly and dangerous task which the chef-de-train allotted to the most junior member of this staff. He came back into the train half frozen, and had to be thawed out by his colleagues in front of the kitchen stove. But at least he had been able to report that the snow was no longer falling, and this was good news welcomed by one and all, train crew and passengers alike.

Inside the wagon-lits and the parlour-car it was comparatively warm, for the individual stoves were kept well charged. Passengers, however, were becoming bored; boredom made them irritable; and irritability led to arguments and, sometimes, hard words. The young English courier had a habit of whistling tunelessly through his teeth for what seemed to his unappreciative fellow-passengers hours on end. Several nationalities were represented in the close confines of the parlour-car, and inevitably matters of politics and religion cropped up, which led to warm argument and conflicts of opinion that hovered dangerously close, sometimes, to conflicts of a more physical kind. The chef-de-train had more than once to intervene and smooth down ruffled feelings and calm hot tempers.

Menus became less varied, and portions served at table considerably smaller. There were no second helpings. Though wine was still served, it was by the glass rather than a bottle at a time for each passenger. The general standard of the meals deteriorated, though every dish continued to be served with the care and precision and attention to detail that always characterised the restaurant-car staff. The chef-de-train paid his regular and frequent visits to satisfy himself that all the passengers under his care were being as well looked after as the circumstances made possible.

One day it became unpleasantly obvious that the temperature in the cars had dropped far below the level to which the passengers were accustomed: the steam-heating had had to be drastically curtailed. Passengers took to wearing their greatcoats throughout the day. The lucky ones who had rugs with them made good use of them; those who had not, borrowed the blankets off their bunks and unashamedly wrapped them round their feet and knees, or draped them round their shoulders as they huddled in their seats. Others retired to their bunks, covered their blankets with their greatcoats, and kept warm that way, emerging only to eat their meals. Standards were deteriorating rapidly.

Soon, meals were reduced to one per day, and even that was not the sort of meal ordinarily served aboard the Orient Express. Worse, the steam-heating dropped to a level so low as to be almost non-existent. When protests were made, and it was pointed out that low temperatures could result in pneumonia, and even death, the chef-de-train answered gravely that the supplies of fuel kept for stoking the individual stoves were now completely exhausted, and though there was some coal in the tender it was of a type that could not be burned in the stoves because it required a forced draught. The little fuel that remained, he said firmly, must be conserved for use in the kitchen, otherwise there would be no more hot meals, not even any more hot coffee to keep up their spirits. Within the next twenty-four hours the chef-de-train, whose customary rubicund face was now grey and haggard with worry, told them, there might not be enough fuel left even for that.

'Then a party had better be sent out to look for wood to replace the used fuel,' said the courier. 'If no one else will do so, I will lead the party myself!'

There was a murmur of appreciation from the other passengers, but this was quickly stilled when the chef-de-train spoke once more: 'There are more than three metres of snow on each side of the train,' he said, looking at him gravely. 'It has made a roof right over the Orient Express. But for that, you might, messieurs les voyageurs, be even colder than you are. It is one small thing, perhaps, for which to be thankful. But it makes a sortie in search of more fuel quite out of the question.'

By now the gas-cylinders that fed the lamps in the train were empty. During the day the coaches were murkily lit by thin daylight filtering through the snow to the windows, now coated with a sheet of ice both inside and out. During the long hours of darkness there was no light at all. The stove in the kitchen sufficed to produce a bowl of soup for each passenger at fairly regular intervals. The last of the wine had gone, so that the warming effect of alcohol was not available any longer to the starved and half-frozen passengers. The chef-de-train kept in reserve a bottle or two of cognac, but these were exclusively for use in emergency, and were locked up by him personally, and he kept the key in his pocket.

It became colder and yet colder. Diplomatically, the chef-de-train removed the thermometer from the end wall of the parlour-car so that his passengers could do no more than guess what the temperature had fallen to. Even inside the train it was well below freezing-point. What it might be outside the train no one liked even to contemplate: thirty degrees of frost, in all probability; perhaps more.

The supply of drinking-water ran out. This, however, was no great problem—at first: snow could always be collected and melted down for water. Not that anyone in the train was interested in drinking water: but it could be used to make hot coffee—so long as the coffee itself held out, and the supply of fuel for the auxiliary kitchen stove. This was a small paraffin-burning stove kept in reserve for emergency: it could do little more than boil a few pans of water, at best.

It was the steady drop in the level of the paraffin-tank—their last reserve—even more than the diminishing supplies of food that promoted a desperate decision. It was obvious that though the railway authorities in Turkey must by now have realised that the train was already long overdue, they were unable to force a way through to rescue them. Therefore, they had only themselves to depend on. Somehow they themselves must make contact with the outside world, or they would all die of starvation or exposure: it was as simple an issue as that; a matter, quite literally, of life or death.

The chef-de-train called a conference of passengers, and put the case briefly to them. There were two alternatives: either they must break out of their prison and, somehow, force their way through the snow until they could obtain help—or, they must all lose their lives. To force their way out would be a gruelling task; but it was one which must succeed—or they must perish in the attempt. He asked for the help of every able-bodied passenger to reinforce his own staff. M. Souf, the Turk, immediately declined. Fräulein von Werner, of course, was excused; as were two or three of the more elderly male passengers. But that left a labour force of a dozen and more, a mixture of passengers and train staff.

The plan was to tunnel outwards from the train. The tunnel would be started on the leeward side, not because there was any certainty that that would bring them soonest to some habitation but because the snow might be expected to be less thick on that side than the windward side. They must dig hard enough to cut a channel into the open, and simply hope and pray that they were digging in the right direction. The train carried a small amount of equipment: a few shovels, a pick-axe or two, and some iron bars. These must suffice. There must be an advance gang, equipped with these tools; and they must be supported by reserves who would clear away the snow they cut, and take their places on a rota when the advance party became exhausted.

So, they began. Work started beside the locomotive, where the warmth of the slowly dying fire had kept the snow clear for a few feet. The diggers worked outwards at right angles from this point: outwards and slightly upwards, too, so that they could carve their way through the roof of snow and thus be able to dispose of the snow, throwing it clear of the narrow track they were cutting.

It was slow and very strenuous work, for the snow had now lain so long that it was packed hard and firm. Beneath their feet it was soon stamped down to the consistency of ice. The men with the picks soon became exhausted and had to be replaced by others who had not had such hard work to do. The chef-de-train organised the rota in such a way that there were always at least two men up in front who were rested and fresh. But it was so bitterly cold that when a man's job was temporarily over he had to find a means of keeping himself warm or he might well be afflicted with frostbite.

At length the pick-and-shovel brigade broke through to the surface; now what had been a tunnel roofed over with snow could be turned into a channel. The ice-cold air caused them to catch their breaths in pain, and they bent to their task with more determination than ever.

After a good many hours' furious digging there was a despairing shout from behind them; the men at the snow-face looked back, to see that the walls and roof of the tunnel they had been cutting had caved in behind them. All that snow débris would have to be shovelled away before they could get back to the train at the end of their day's digging! The chef-de-train organised a party to clear the tunnel while the others went ahead. As soon as a way back to the train had been cleared he told some of his gang to go and wrench off the steps and running-boards and any other timber they could prise loose, so as to buttress the sides of the tunnel against further collapse. Twice more those walls caved in before the timber could be wedged in position; but under his inspiring leadership the workers never entirely lost heart.

For two long days and well into each night, when they could carry on working beneath the strong light of a mocking silvery moon, the gangs laboured at their task, hacking away at the endless wall of snow confronting them, trampling it down to make a firm and solid foot-way, throwing the snow clear to keep it from falling in on them again. Their hands were blistered, their shoulder and arm muscles ached, sometimes they felt as though they were breathing in fire, so icy cold was the air that entered their lungs. But they fought their way ever farther and farther from the train, still hidden from them beneath its whale-back blanket of thick snow. The handful of passengers cooped up in the train, dependent on the able-bodied if there was to be any chance of ultimate rescue, willingly cut down on their already slender ration of hot coffee to enable the workers to fortify themselves at their expense; they certainly deserved all they got, little as it inevitably was.

Mercifully the snow held off. Once or twice it threatened, and the hearts of the labouring gang fell at the prospect. But after a flurry or two the sky cleared again and they felt reprieved. Then, quite unexpectedly, came the first really hopeful sign. As dusk fell, a few lights became visible far away across the frozen, snow-blanketed landscape: the first they had seen. Where there were lights there must be people, they told one another excitedly; and where there were people—there must be food! With hope once more in their hearts they bent again to their task, and with renewed vigour, swinging their picks and shovels. The English diplomatic courier, who had worked as hard as anyone, began again whistling tunelessly between his teeth, and for once no one made any protest.

When the moon dropped and darkness fell they had to give up their digging; but next morning at first light they were digging away harder than ever, for they felt now that the end of their trials was in sight. The chef-de-train had had a sledge constructed out of pieces of wood torn from one of the fourgons: as soon as practicable a party would hitch themselves to it and fight their way towards where those lights had been seen. All hands were now working harder than ever, for they were increasingly convinced that victory was in sight.

At last the time came when the chef-de-cuisine and two sturdy members of the train staff harnessed themselves to the makeshift sledge and set out boldly for the village, whose roof-tops could now just be seen pricking through the snow in the light of the rising sun. Plunging thigh-deep in patches of soft snow and alternately jerking on to ledges of close-packed, harder snow, dragging their sledge behind them, they staggered forward at their best possible pace, their noses lifted to the promise of food ahead.

Unhappily, the welcome they received at the village was very different from what they had fondly hoped it would be. It was a very small village indeed, hardly more than a cluster of tumbledown hovels sheltered from the full fury of the blizzard by a half-circle of stunted trees. Its poverty-stricken inhabitants had been driven to extremes by the isolation they suffered when deep snow cut off all communication with any other communities in that vast and dreary stretch of empty country. They themselves, they declared, were practically starving. Certainly they had nothing to spare for the strangers who had so unexpectedly turned up in their midst.

But these same strangers, who had fought their way from the train across the snowy waste to the village, were desperate men, and in the mood for taking desperate measures. Hunger, before all else, quells a man's scruples. While the chef talked hard, and incomprehensibly, to the small group of villagers who had emerged, startled, from the low and narrow doorways of their hovels and were now listening curiously to words whose meaning at least was plain enough, his subordinates were doing a quick scrounge round behind their backs.

They gathered up a few eggs, and even managed to snatch up a scrawny hen or two and thrust these into sacks while gripping their necks to muffle their strangled cries. They snatched up, too, such fragments of wood as they could lay their hands on, and broke off the lower branches from the trees surrounding the village and loaded these on to their sledge. Then, pursued by Turkish maledictions that seemed to make the icy air sizzle round their ears, they retraced their steps as fast as they could, heading for the security of their stranded train before they were manhandled and injured by the angry villagers. At any moment, they believed, they might hear gun-shots behind them, and find themselves attacked in the rear.

Once back on board the train, and their precious spoils shared out as fairly as possible, what amounted to a council of war was held. Considering their efforts and their high hopes, the sortie had been disappointing in the extreme. They would, it was quite clear, have to try again; and succeed better this time than last!

Starvation is an ugly word, and it hung in the air among them throughout their discussion. There was not a single passenger or member of the train staff who was not feeling, and showing, the effects of deprivation and cold. Some bore it more stoically than others; some seemed to have few reserves of courage and faith. Unhappiest of all was poor, pretty Fräulein von Werner. For some time past she had seemed to be in a sort of coma, listlessly unaware of anything that was going on around her. She had retired to her bunk and lay there day and night, speechless, or moaning softly as though in a nightmare.

One night as the conducteur made his routine round he heard a scream from the compartment she occupied on her own. Snatching at his pass-key, he threw open the door and looked in. By the light of the candle-lamp he carried he saw blood flowing from a white wrist that hung over the side of her bunk, thin as that of a skeleton. In her despair, her mind temporarily unhinged by her fears of what might be going to happen, Fräulein von Werner had broken off a corner of her mirror and slashed an artery with it; she no longer had the will or even the desire to live. Perhaps she held some secret in her heart that she had not communicated to anyone. The conducteur was just in time to seize a bandage from the first-aid kit and apply a swift tourniquet to her forearm before she bled to death.

The net result of the council of war was quite simply this: food *must* be obtained, and at no matter what cost. The only known source of supply seemed to be that village. The only way of extracting sufficient food from the villagers, since stealing was out of the question (the chef-de-train had had to register an official protest about the petty pilfering that had taken place on that first visit), was to offer the villagers so much money that in their astonishment and greed they would forget their own situation. Half-measures would not be enough: they must be dazzled with the promise of wealth. Money, observed the chef-de-train, 'talks'; especially gold! And this would mean a whip-round among the passengers.

So, once again a party set out along the tunnel and on to the beaten track beyond it. This time it was led by the chef-de-train himself, the ultimate authority. Two members of the party, on his instructions, carried shot-guns with them, wrapped in cloths so that it was not obvious what they were, but available in the event of possible trouble. They could not be certain that this second visit of theirs would not be met with hostility: by now the villagers would no doubt have realised that some of their eggs and hens had in fact been stolen during the visit of the day before.

The party were spotted by look-outs long before they reached the village. When they came close enough it could be seen that some of the villagers were carrying firearms, and it was a comfort to know that they had guns of their own, though they hoped it would not prove necessary to use them.

The chef-de-train spoke several languages, including Turkish, though he did not speak the outlandish dialect of these villagers. However, he spoke enough to be able to make it quite clear that he and his party had come with good intentions. They had brought with them, he emphasised, offerings. The armed villagers lowered their ancient and dangerous-looking firearms, but still kept them at the ready while they waited to see what was forthcoming.

To their astonishment they saw what was forthcoming: gold coin; gold in plenty; more gold than any of them had ever seen in their lives before. They were quick to realise that here was an unprecedented opportunity for gain; and gain on their own terms, however stiff they might like to make them. Boorish as they might be, they had a peasant shrewdness. They had the wit to realise that here was a party of desperate men, men completely at their mercy. It was a situation they had never known before, a situation which would probably never again confront them. They must make the most of it.

'I have not come to haggle, but to buy,' said the chef-de-train. He knew that he must speak boldly and persuasively, or lose the throw.

The villagers were staggered. Not come to haggle? Why, never in their whole lives before had they obtained anything they wanted without a preliminary bout of haggling; it was the way all transactions were carried out in their part of the world, and always had been. Their eyes never left the display of coin that the chef-de-train spread out before them, glittering in the light of the cold morning sunshine. They completely forgot their own hunger. They had come near enough to starvation in the past, many times, when winters such as this had befallen them. They had survived, and would survive this time, too. And on those previous occasions they had not had gold displayed before them to give them heart!

Eggs? Why, of course! Eggs were promptly fetched from within the poverty-stricken hovels where the women-folk were immured with their stock, curiously speculating as to what was going on outside. The chef-de-train offered to buy as many as the village could produce, and at any price the headman might care to demand. The headman placed a price on each individual egg that no good French housewife would have dreamed of paying for half a gross of eggs; and the chef-de-train paid for them—in gold, as promised.

Hens? Why, of course! There were plenty of hens in the village. Every household had its own small flock, sharing the warmth of the hovel with its owners. The chef-de-train demanded to be shown a specimen or two. They were brought out for him to look over: poor, scrawny creatures, mere bundles of bedraggled feathers that looked as though they had not more than an ounce or two of stringy flesh on their bones among them. The price asked for them was outrageous, but the chef-de-train paid it without a murmur; the very lives of his passengers were at stake and he could not afford to protest.

Meanwhile, the chef, who of course knew more about food than anyone else, was becoming increasingly impatient. How far would a dozen, even a score, of hens such as these go among his ever-increasingly hungry passengers? Something more solid than hens and eggs was urgently necessary. He muttered as much to the chef-de-train, who nodded, as much as to indicate that he had by no means finished yet.

Sheep, or goats? Why, of course! The headman spoke to some of his fellow villagers, and they scurried away, to return soon afterwards with some of the most miserable-looking specimens ever seen in an open market. But the chef-de-train knew that beggars could not afford to be choosers. He contrived not to register his real feelings at the astronomical sum demanded by the headman for each scraggy specimen, take-it-or-leave-it. Fortified by the chef-de-cuisine at his side, he took it. And as he did so, the chef at his elbow muttered: 'And we can't eat them raw, remember!'

Now, fuel? Why, of course! once more came the eager response. A sledge was borrowed from one of the villagers and piled high with logs already cut to length for the wood-burning stoves in use in their homes. They cost almost their weight in gold, it seemed; but they were worth this to the chef-de-train and his starving, half-frozen passengers. The sledge was piled high with logs lashed down with straw ropes. The makeshift sledge they had brought with them, too, was piled high with the provisions they had bought at such outrageous prices. How much more successful their second mission had been!

Now the foraging party, with its two sledges, and a couple of sheep and two goats on the hoof, set off on their return journey to the still-buried train. One or two of them glanced back over their shoulders from time to time, not wholly trusting those rapacious villagers, half anticipating that even now they might raise their antiquated guns to their shoulders and shoot them down as they trudged over the path they had beaten in the snow, their backs now turned to the village. However, those villagers had already begun squabbling over their individual shares in the booty that had so unexpectedly come their way, and were far too engrossed in their arguments to take any further notice of the strangers who had left so much unexpected coin in their hands.

But the foraging party, already congratulating itself on its success, was not out of trouble yet. Danger once more threatened them, and from a wholly unexpected quarter. Probably excited by the smell of sheep and goats, a small pack of wolves appeared from a clump of trees and headed at a brisk, purposeful lope in their direction. Now real disaster threatened! Every member of the party knew that nothing would baulk a starving wolf in search of prey. Thank God they had had the foresight to bring guns with them when they set out for the village!

The guns were in the hands of the fireman and the chef, two men who happened to be expert shots. And on this vital occasion they certainly proved their expertise. Crack! Crack! They had waited only until the pack had slowed down to a stealthy, furtive, creeping approach before they fired. The two shots were well aimed: the pack leader and its second tumbled over in the snow, jerked convulsively, and then lay still, patches of blood spilling out on to the snow and immediately congealing there. The remainder of the pack, frightened, hesitated and were dispersed by two more shots from the marksmen. They turned tail and raced back into the trees from which they had so menacingly appeared a few minutes before. The chef and the fireman plunged across the snow to make sure that the two victims were well and truly dead, and then called for assistance to load them on to the sledge. After all, the chef-de-cuisine remarked, were wolf-steaks a dish to be despised by starving men?

Back at the train, they were greeted with a heroes' welcome. Now things began to look up. With careful husbanding of their new resources there was a reasonable prospect of survival for several days to come. And inside that time, surely a relief-party would have succeeded in forcing a way through to them from one direction or another? As a matter of fact the chef-de-train had done more than merely negotiate for food and fuel. While this had been loading on to the sledges he had got the village headman to promise to send two of his hardiest villagers cross-country by horse-drawn sleigh to the nearest point from which help might be obtained. In such appalling conditions, he had been told, the journey might take as much as two days; but—it would be made. That, the headman, greedy for a personal reward which he need not share, faithfully promised.

And he fulfilled his promise. Three days later a member of the train staff on watch duty yelled that a convoy of six sleighs was approaching them. When they had come close enough he reported that they were a detachment of Turkish soldiery. They arrived with a tremendous flourish, bringing with them provisions and fuel galore. They brought with them, too, the heartening news that a break-down unit comprising a huge gang of railwaymen in a special wagon, with a snow-plough outfit mounted on the front of the most powerful locomotive the Turkish Railways could provide, was now fighting its way westwards along the line to rescue the marooned train. Within a day or two at most, they said, it should be within hailing distance.

The information brought new hope and courage to even the most despondent of the passengers. Heartened by it, the more able-bodied among them, the original pick-and-shovel brigade, threw themselves cheerfully into the monumental task of freeing the engine and tender, the wagon-lits and wagon-salon-restaurant, from the icy grip of the snow packed hard up against it and jammed between its bogies and undercarriage. Working like beavers, with the promise of rescue so near at hand, they freed a length of track immediately ahead of 'le Ten-Wheel'.

With every yard of track cleared they knew they were that much closer to their longed-for rescue. The driver and fireman got up steam in their locomotive, knowing that a further supply of briquettes would be coming up with the break-down gang. And the glorious moment came when the distant smoke they had seen hanging darkly over the snow-covered track to the east proved, as they had hoped and prayed, to be that of the big locomotive struggling westwards through the deep snow towards them behind the giant snow-plough mounted in front of it.

Now, over the silent waste land of snow they could actually hear the deep-throated pulsing of the engine as it drew nearer and nearer to them. It was a long time before it came fully into their view, for the snow was still deep on the track and the great masses of snow thrown up by the plough made a screen in front of it, a man-made concentrated snow-storm. The loose snow was banked up high to right and left of the engine and plough, threatening all the time to topple down and obliterate the entire break-down unit as it struggled towards them.

The diggers working ahead of the marooned train redoubled their efforts, far too excited to do the sensible thing and relax while the snow-plough did their work for them. They wanted, after all this time, to have an actual share in their own rescue.

At long last, shovellers and snow-plough met, rescuers and rescued could shake hands and embrace. The more ebullient passengers, the Frenchmen, did just that. The Turks were their brothers! '*Vive la Turquie!*' they cried, and threw their arms about one another.

Less ebullient, characteristically British and reserved, the English diplomatic courier shook hands with their rescuers and muttered some halting words of thanks. A Moslem passenger, none other than M. Souf, dropped to his knees on a patch that had been cleared of snow and faced in the direction he now knew to be true east, the direction in which Mecca lay. Silently he lowered himself and touched the icy earth with his forehead in worship.

The interminable ordeal was over. Steam was raised, fuel supplies replenished, wheels turned once more. Good news had been brought by the rescue party: farther back down the line over which they had fought their way the snow was less than it was in the midway stretch, near Tcherkeuy. No more snow was falling. The track was now reasonably clear right through to the Bosporus.

And so, more than a week behind schedule, the Orient Express at last trundled into the station, its long and memorable journey at an end. During that final stage the passengers got together to consider how best to show their gratitude to the chef-de-train for the way he had looked after them throughout their terrible ordeal. They would all, of course, give him and the rest of the train staff the handsome *pourboires* that were the usual practice aboard this luxury train. But they wanted to do something more than that—something more personal altogether.

Eventually, after much discussion, they decided that some sort of a testimonial would be the best thing: a testimonial that would be signed by every one of them individually. It would express their gratitude in a personal way. It would place on record their combined appreciation of the thought and courage and faith and encouragement in adverse circumstances that he had manifested throughout their ordeal. Perhaps it would give him pleasure to keep it, as a permanent souvenir of a grim episode in which he had played such an outstanding part. It would be so drafted as to include reference to the members of the train staff who had served them all so devotedly under his inspiration. It read:

> We passengers aboard the Simplon-Orient feel it our duty to place on record the fact that the entire staff of the train marooned in the snow near Tcherkesskeuy for five long days, and in the most appalling conditions, individually made superhuman efforts to ensure that their passengers should suffer the least possible discomfort. At great risk to themselves they climbed on to the roofs of the coaches, amid the full force of the blizzard, to obtain water for us; and though short of all that was essential, individually did their duty by us to the bitter end.
>
> Tcherkesskeuy, 5th February, 1929

Every passenger signed the statement, which was duly presented to the chef-de-train a few minutes before they arrived at their destination. It is curious that no mention was made of the major feature of the whole adventure: the breaking out from the marooned train and foraging for provisions that, most surely, saved their lives. But certainly the gesture gave great pleasure to the chef-de-train. He treasured the small document during the remainder of his service, and it was among his proudest souvenirs to show to his friends during the long years of an honourable and well-earned retirement.

12

Death of a Train

The testimonial to that gallant chef-de-train carried the words 'Simplon-Express', not 'Orient Express'. This may seem puzzling, for after all, the famous train had been established forty-six years by then and it might be thought that passengers would have been familiar with its name. But it was not quite so simple a matter as that.

When, some fifteen years before the inaugural run of the Orient Express, the world's first transcontinental train, the famous 'Union Pacific', was inaugurated, to link the Atlantic coast of America with the Pacific, it passed, of course, through a number of individual states, such as Nebraska, Wyoming, Utah, Nevada and California. But these states were all 'united' beneath the stars and stripes of the United States of America. It was a very different matter, however, when the Compagnie Internationale des Wagons-Lits et des Grands Express Européens set about establishing a trans-European railway system. For this involved the crossing of a number of frontiers between the sovereign states that constituted the continent of Europe.

No other continent in the world has seen so many changes in the first half of this century as Europe has done.

There have been the relatively minor 'Balkan Wars'; there have been two major wars, one lasting from 1914 until 1918, the other from 1939 until 1945. Inevitably, loyalties and jealousies between the countries involved in these wars produced problems which hit the transcontinental railway system where it hurt most. Frontiers were closed; lengths of railway-track were torn up, or rendered so dangerous that it would have been folly for any railway company to send its trains over them. All long-distance trains were affected; and none of them worse than the Orient Express.

It 'died' the first time on the eve of the outbreak of the First World War. At that time it was ending the period of its heyday, when it had been running four times weekly from Paris to Constantinople and back, and three times weekly to Constantza and back. It was not given the kiss of life again until 1919.

But even then it had to be re-routed over a considerable part of its journey because of the confusion as to frontiers and the aftermath of hostilities; it had to avoid passing over any German or Austrian territory. So, it now ran through the famous Simplon Tunnel, that wonderful twelve-mile-long tunnel hewn out of the Alps that soar between Brig, in Switzerland, and Domodossola in Italy. To mark this change to a new route, the original Orient Express now had the name 'Simplon' tacked on to it. For convenience, the triple-barrelled name was often shortened to either 'Simplon-Express' or (preferably) 'Simplon-Orient'. The first of these was the name that appeared on the testimonial signed by those grateful passengers in February, 1929.

Later there was another change of route in the earlier,

Western European stages. Peace had been more or less established in Europe. Though some frontiers had been changed topographically, most of them had been re-opened to long-distance traffic. The Orient Express was re-routed again. This time its route was much closer to its original one than that of the Simplon-Orient, which had dipped as far south as northern Italy and passed through Milan and Mestre (near Venice), Trieste and Zagreb.

The new route, established in 1932, just over half a century since the birth of the famous train, passed from France into Switzerland, but instead of then continuing southwards into Italy, as the Simplon-Orient had done, turned northwards by way of the six-mile-long Arlberg Tunnel and Austria once again, and thence eastwards as before. It therefore had the name 'Arlberg' prefixed to it.

Once again a major war broke out; once again these great transcontinental trains were brought to a halt. The first of these to be put into commission again, only four months after the cessation of hostilities, was the Arlberg-Orient Express, though for some time it did not cover the whole of the route over which it had been scheduled to run.

Unhappily, the cessation of hostilities did not mean, as some optimists had hoped and even believed, that henceforward there was going to be complete freedom for people to move at will about the Continent, as they had been able to do in the glorious heyday of the original Orient Express. Rumblings of discontent among the nations that had been involved on one side or the other during World War Two became louder and louder. There were 'incidents' at frontiers that ought to have been open to long-distance travellers. In 1951, almost without warning, Turkey closed her frontier with Bulgaria. This meant that the

Paris–Istanbul (Constantinople's new name) express could no longer make the through journey; it had to turn back either at Sofia or at Svilengrad. If a passenger was determined to get through to Istanbul by rail he had to take a new and circuitous route that passed through Yugoslavia and Greece. In 1952 yet another route to Istanbul was found, by way of Salonika.

Meanwhile Czechoslovakia had turned Communist, which meant that she did everything in her power to seal herself off from non-Communist countries. Her internal rail services broke down and contracts of long standing were torn up as though they were waste paper. More sinister than anything that happened up to that time was the moment when the first shadows of the so-called 'Iron Curtain' began to fall over Europe. This was a new and quite unpredictable menace to long-distance communication by rail, and these great trains, the glorified descendants, as it were, of the first Orient Express that had trundled two thousand miles across Europe behind the gallant little 'Est' 2—4—0, were among the first victims. Again there had to be re-routing. Desperate attempts were made to maintain the established tradition of safe, swift and punctual services between Western Europe and the fringe of the Orient. But anyone with his eyes open could easily see that the great days of such travel were coming to their end.

There was another, and more insidious, threat to the continuance of railway travel: the airplane. An airplane could virtually ignore frontiers. Where a train might reach an occasional speed of sixty miles an hour, and average perhaps fifty miles an hour (exclusive of stops) over two or three hundred miles of central European territory, an airplane could travel at ten times that speed, and maintain that speed from start to finish of its scheduled flight. A train might take sixty hours and more between Paris and Istanbul; an airplane could do the journey in less than one-tenth that time.

There were no Customs posts to pass through at frontiers, no language problems continually cropping up as the passenger moved out of one country and into the next. The journey was simple, straightforward, and expeditious. It was, admittedly, a good deal more expensive than the train journey had been, at least in the old days; but what was paid out in cash was saved in time, convenience and comfort. The development of the international airlines network finally spelled the doom of the Orient Express that, with a break or two resulting from two major wars, had reigned supreme in Europe for something like eighty years.

Until May, 1962, the Arlberg-Orient Express included one solitary wagon-lits from Paris as far east as Bucharest; after that month it ran only as far as Vienna, and forfeited the proud name 'Orient'. Until the same month of the same year the Simplon-Orient continued to run on a skeleton bi-weekly service from Paris to Istanbul; but the train was only a ghost of its former self.

On the 27th May, 1962, the Orient Express—died.

For almost eighty years it had been a name to conjure with. It had fired the imaginations of scores of writers: writers not only of thrillers and whodunits but of poems to its glory, men like the French poet Valéry Larbaud, who had written eloquently of the luxury train's 'silent gliding across a slumbering Europe, in whose compartments sleep *les millionnaires*'.

It was another Frenchman, Paul Morand, who wrote the obsequies of the fabulous train, briefly, but with true feeling. He echoed what everyone has felt who knew the train in its great days; what every chef-de-train and conducteur has felt, and placed on record, even if not in such eloquent and moving terms:

> The Orient Express has vanished, destroyed by the 100-seater airplane. The very society for which the train was created has itself died. Passports and visas, frontier changes and the new 'Wall of China' (the Iron Curtain) have brought this about. No longer shall there be those long days and nights aboard a train crossing a continent that can now be crossed in two hours. No more international trains; instead, a coach or two tacked on to some local train and then tacked on to another for the next stretch of the journey. The world of Diplomacy, the world of Big Business, the world of Luxury hardly knows of the existence of trains. Even ships are but little more than propaganda fiction. Luxury today takes off at Orly Airport, London Airport, Zurich, Idlewild. . . .
>
> So, on the tomb of the Orient Express let us now lay, by way of a commemorative wreath, a propellor and airplane seat; let the Great Train rest in peace!

Index

ENGLISH CHANNEL
NETHER
BELGIUM
RHINE
G E R
MARNE
PARIS
SEINE
LX
Vitry le François
Nancy
F R A N C E
Strasbourg
Stuttgart
DANUBE
Ulm
Augsburg
Munich
SWITZERLAND
Salzbu
A U S
RHONE
SPAIN
I T A L Y
CORSICA
ROME
SARDINIA
M E D I T E R R A N E A N
SICILY
A F R I C A